ENGAGING
THE HEART
UNDERSTANDING THE TREASURE WITHIN

ENGAGING THE HEART
UNDERSTANDING THE TREASURE WITHIN

GAIL MCWILLIAMS

ENGAGING THE HEART

© 2008 Gail McWilliams

Written by Gail McWilliams

Cover Design and Graphics: Ryan Duckworth
Photography: Andrea Calvery and Ryan Duckworth

All rights reserved. No part of this publication may be reproduced, stored in any retrieval system, or transmitted in any form or by any means, mechanical, photocopying, recording, or otherwise, without permission in writing from the publisher, except by a reviewer, who may quote brief passages in a review.

Manufactured in the United States of America.

For information, please contact:

Generations Global Press
PO Box 765127
Dallas, Texas 75376-5127

www.GenerationsGlobal.com
888-270-0182

"…beyond the horizon, around the globe and to generations yet to come."

Paperback ISBN: 978-0-9799512-2-0
LCCN: 2008911237
1 2 3 4 5 6 7 8 9 10

All scripture quotations, unless otherwise indicated, are taken from the New King James Version. ®
Copyright © 1982 by Thomas Nelson, Inc.
Used by permission. All rights reserved.

DEDICATION

To the many who have asked,
"How did you train your children to guard their heart?"

Table of Contents
Engaging the Heart

Acknowledgements viii

Preface: From the Stroller x

Introduction: Game of Hearts xiv

Chapter One
    Who Has Your Heart? 1

Chapter Two
    Cup of Purity 7

Chapter Three
    The Blessing 14

Chapter Four
    Sleeping Beauty 23

Chapter Five
    Secret Garden 31

Chapter Six
    The Impostor 35

TABLE OF CONTENTS

Chapter Seven
    No Secrets — No Lies..45

Chapter Eight
    Crowded Altar..54

Chapter Nine
    Heart Strings...67

Chapter Ten
    The Exchange..76

Chapter Eleven
    The Kiss..89

Chapter Twelve
    Covenant Love...99

Chapter Thirteen
    King of Hearts...108

Chapter Fourteen
    Is It Too Late?...116

End Notes..123

About the Author...141

Acknowledgements

Special thanks go to…

My husband Tony. You gave up your time and projects at hand to help me accomplish my second book. Your selfless overtures of laying down your own book project to help finish mine were a priceless gift. Your attention to detail and solid doctrine kept me on track. I could not have written the book without your eyes and skills. Thank you.

Lydia and Connor. Once more you shared your lives with others so that I could write around the clock. Thank you for your patience and acceptance of the assignment for this hour. You are the best and your stories added so much in the book. My favorite times were when we sat around our table to read a chapter aloud and get your feedback. Thank you for your great reviews.

Anna, Lindey and Holly. Thank you for being the first to read the manuscript and sign off on it. Your opinions and permission to use your lives and stories added to the collection of a diverse compilation of seasons and teaching. Without all of my children, the book would have been missing its heart.

Mom and Dad. With every book or important piece of writing I am grateful to my first string of editors close to my heart—my parents. Mom and Dad, thank you for always being willing to review, check grammar and offer helpful suggestions. I am so proud of you, with both of you being in your mid-seventies, for even knowing how to

Acknowledgements

use a computer, not to mention, keeping it running around the clock with rewrites and edits. Don't ever retire; we need you. Dad, your scriptural references at the end of my books add so much. Thanks for the long hours you searched for passages I referenced.

Ryan. Thank you for your artistic skills and cutting edge ideas that have made me stretch. I love your heart and willingness to serve. How great of the Lord to give us a wonderfully skilled son-in-law.

Anna Jean Price. Thank you for your extra editing eyes and endless encouragement.

All who reviewed the book. Thank you for your comments and for your time and your insight. You were an encouraging test market.

All who took the time and effort to write an endorsement. Thank you.

Those who gave me permission to use their name. I am grateful for your letting us read a short page from your life-story.

Though we were not afforded a three-month sabbatical or a monetary advance for stopping regular life to go away and write the book, God did place us in some great locations as we toted our manuscript from one state in the nation to another. Bruce and Julie, thanks for loaning us your beautiful home, nestled away in the woods of Michigan, for a few weeks. Oklahoma country manors to Georgia apartments, coffee shops and hotel rooms became reading and rereading corners as we reviewed and reread *Engaging the Heart*. Each time, I could only think of you—the reader and the generations yet to come. I wept over your broken hearts and smiled at those who remained pure. I am sobered to think that the hearts held in the balance will be determined by a choice.

Preface
From the Stroller

Nestled in the Appalachian Mountains, near Billy Graham's home, is Montreat, North Carolina. It was late one spring that my husband, Tony, and I traveled there to the foot of Black Mountain to attend a National Leadership Conference. We were young and new to parenting. Our firstborn daughter, Anna, was nine months old at the time. She sat quietly during the sessions in her umbrella stroller while we were challenged and inspired as young leaders with new responsibilities. Never did I dream a decision that week would direct our family course for years to come.

Sitting on the right side of the auditorium in the balcony, we listened to the evening guest speaker from Dallas, Texas. I don't remember his text, except for a story about raising his children and their values. He stated, "When our daughter is pursued by a young gentleman, he must go through me first."

Laughter broke out, as he continued in sincerity. He next told about his son who recently had begun dating. The young man had called the young lady's father and asked permission to date his daughter. Now, the crowd sat attentively. By asking permission, the young man showed value for the daughter and gained the father's immediate respect. We were impressed.

A seed was planted in our minds to consider something more than just typical routine dating. This one simple example from his

Preface: From the Stroller

message immediately resonated deep within us. We simultaneously looked at each other, saying aloud, "We will do the same!" Treasuring our own daughter, we agreed that moment to value the guarding of her heart. In spite of our idealism, our hearts were impacted and open to further search out the matter in the days and years ahead. The seed sown that night, which has been developing over many years, has since grown and influenced our evolving journey. In time, it became apparent our quest was not for some ironclad list of rules but, instead, for principles that would protect and guard the heart and its issues.

What ages do you begin teaching about relationships? Why is the heart so important? Is purity a choice or a process? What makes the difference? Who will protect your heart?

In the middle of rising divorce rates, broken hearts and dissolved relationships, one can't help but ask, "Is there a more excellent way?" Consequently, deliberate decisions have been made in our family about purity and keeping the heart. That one decision so many years ago is now one of the deep pier beams of the foundation of our home.

Proverbs 4:23 says, "Keep your heart with all diligence, for out of it spring the issues of life." Too much is at stake. Issues of the heart affect every aspect of our lives. Issues are more than just a buzz term psychologists have made famous. The Lord told us about safeguards that would keep toxins, debris and impurity from stealing away our hearts, protecting them at all costs.

Choices of the heart are individual, which include knowing the love of the Savior and His forgiveness. However, by default or intentionally, we pave our children's future paths by erecting landmarks etched with our own conduct and standards, often with no thought of generations yet to come.

Parents sometimes shrug off raising their children with higher standards than those with which they were raised, saying, "I turned out all right. What's the problem?" Is it pride or is it indifference that keeps us from involving ourselves in the heart issues of our children? Do we fear our own inadequacies will be exposed? Passivity on the part of parents to address relationships falsely assumes their children will make the best choices to survive in their culture. There is much more to life than just surviving. Just because you may have navigated the road of emotions and passion without being scarred or entrapped does not guarantee the next generation will be so successful. Though principles concerning the heart remain constant, our children are facing a culture that is swiftly changing.

Our lives must be the ceiling from which the next generation will build — one of excellence. Excellence is never perfection, however. The difference is that perfection determines there is only one right way, but excellence says, "Surely, there is a better way." And then, with children by our side, we begin to search for it.

Proverbs 2:11 says, "Understanding will keep you." Rules alone can be the breeding grounds for rebellion. Understanding, however, begins and builds on principles that endure the changing winds of influence. A foundation of Biblical truth is essential. More than just providing standards to live by, understanding also enables eyes to see clearly in a world growing dim with compromise.

Pleasure is seasonal and living for self creates a "my space" culture. Such is the case with relationships and dating. Is there more?

What about the years that follow the dating season? How do you

Preface: From the Stroller

recapture your heart once it has been given away? Emotional affairs are just as dangerous as physical affairs because both impact the heart. In time, hearts filled with rejection, unresolved wounds and fantasies may open doors to corresponding and destructive actions.

The Lord wisely explained that hating someone with your heart is equivalent to murder. Lusting after another is no different than carrying out the illegitimate affection for someone whose heart does not belong to you. Proverbs 23:7 exposes the heart, saying, "As a man thinks in his heart, so is he."

One defining choice made while our firstborn was in her stroller has influenced our family and countless others. After five children, and now grandchildren, we have been walking that expanded road and have experienced the benefits of applying the Biblical principles of guarding your heart.

This is not a self-help book or a procedures manual for love and marriage. It is, instead, a book to challenge us to find a more excellent way that goes beyond our former mindsets and commonly accepted practices. My desire is to stimulate discussion and thought as you begin to consider the heart and its issues.

Introduction
Game of Hearts

In the summer fun of vacations and special visits to her grandparents, one day late in the afternoon a little girl heard a familiar sound she had awaited. Her grandfather was finally home. His long day in the mines now seemed brightened by this ray of sunshine that danced on his porch in anticipated joy. She had heard the sounds of his coming home as he turned onto the long gravel driveway at the farm.

Throwing the door open and being the first to meet him on the porch, the game of hearts began. Dancing with feet of anticipation and swirling on the large cement porch, the little girl waited for the routine greeting of exchanged love.

Opening his truck door, her grandpa cheerfully yelled, "Who is the prettiest girl in the world?" Skipping down the path, she confidently yelled back, "Me is, Grandpa! Me is!" Lovingly picking her up with his hard-working arms and now twirling together in the dance, he asked louder, "Who is the prettiest girl in the world?" Answering with giggles and seeming to hear the loving question for the first time, she joyfully said, "Me is, Grandpa. Me is!"

Laughing and with hugs and kisses, he never corrected her poor grammar. His once hard, grim face now softened with smiling eyes and a tender heart of approving love.

Effortlessly, the changing seasons with birthday celebrations

Introduction: Game of Hearts

advanced the clock and surroundings for this little girl.

It was in Mrs. Ward's first grade class that the children merrily took their seats at their small desks to enter the discovery zone of learning. With stories about a boy and girl with their friendly dog, Spot, the reading corner was her favorite. Songs, instruction, coloring, foundational exercises and life skills made a busy school day. The six-year-old elementary girl ran to school expectantly each morning. New friends and endless activities made the days go by quickly. However, one dreaded moment came each Friday afternoon. During clean-up time, the teacher would lead the first graders in a song about loving friends. At the end of the chorus everyone knew to point to the one they liked. Each and every Friday, the young girl would anticipate the upcoming phrase and move fast to jump under her desk to avoid her admirer's choice.

A little boy, with a name too long to spell that tickled her lips to repeat, had set his heart on her. He stood near her to point her out as his choice love. Her speed and nervous anticipation helped her find a safe place under her desk until the song was over, rejecting his desire. She was not for the choosing—not now at least.

As the years advanced, the young school girl, now college-age, endured the upheavals of young love, infatuation, changing hormones, influencing peers, and always looking older than her actual age.

The vibrant young lady's strong leadership skills and deliberate heart for God now seemed of little significance as she drove recklessly down the country road, not caring to live. Her flood of tears blinded her view as she drove toward help late one night. The one she had given her heart to had notified her by phone that their dating relationship was over. He was moving on to find new interests.

Engaging the Heart

Broken by the shattered pieces of a heart fully given to him, she now entertained new thoughts of ending her life. Never before had these desires entered her youthful heart, as she had always been focused on living life to the fullest. However, no pain had ever penetrated her heart like this one. The unrelenting sorrow now overshadowed her life because of one who had uncaringly discarded her like a used toy in search of a new one to hold.

Anger mounted in her, as she tried to counteract the all encompassing pain. With each throbbing impulse she hated herself for being so vulnerable too fast and too young.

It was only mercy that protected her as she drove at fast speeds, now confused and indecisive between ending her life and finding help to start again. After what seemed like hours, she knocked on the front door of a house. A man appeared at the door, the one whom she once had given her heart to years earlier. She had broken his heart, too, when she willfully looked for affections beyond what he could give her. Now, facing him in tears and returning to his protective love, she fell into the arms of her own father, sobbing. Weeping uncontrollably in the safe haven of his arms, she cried, "He said he doesn't love me anymore."

Innocent, young hearts, along with the most experienced, must embrace discernment and discretion. While anticipating true love you may have to boldly resist unwanted suitors, like the little girl who found refuge under her desk. Choosing to open your heart is as challenging as choosing to guard it. How does one safely engage the heart on life's stage with its many characters? Emotionally stimulating scenes and situations with a heart fully open can be dangerous unless boundaries are set by principles.

Proverbs 4:23 wisely reminds us, "Keep your heart with all

Introduction: Game of Hearts

diligence, for out of it spring the issues of life." Have you considered your own heart lately? Who will value it? More important, do you value your own?

Astounding as it may sound, Ecclesiastes 3:11 reveals what your heart is connected to—eternity. Solomon wrote: "He has made everything beautiful in its time. He has also set eternity in the hearts of men; yet they cannot fathom what God has done from beginning to end."

If such a priceless deposit resides within, then who will treasure it?

How will you live—engaging your heart?

Chapter One
Who Has Your Heart?

Many years ago, Tony and I started a Christian school in the Midwest, named "Tree Of Life." It was housed in the church where Tony pastored. It was an exhilarating time seeing hundreds of young children excited to learn. School events which brought their families reminded us we could be a voice in our generation, encouraging households to win.

Our heart had always been to see families succeed, no matter where they were in life. To be entrusted with their children for hours a day and to be privileged to have the opportunity to interlace education with an introduction to the gospel was a rewarding experience, as well as a serious responsibility.

Every Thursday we would have a chapel service for all the student body. With an auditorium filled with vibrant life, Tony would teach character qualities coupled with Bible stories, and I would lead the children in music. It was a favorite day for me. The children, along with the staff, would sing happy songs as they began to learn to worship. Singing the Word of God was my focus because it accomplished two goals at once—worshiping God and learning His word.

With every chapel, the energized crowd would break out with applause and great laughter when my buddies, Dake and Cubby, would appear from behind the grand piano. Though I was the voice and heart of these puppets, I liked it when they came, too.

Engaging the Heart

Cubby, a little bear with innocent eyes, and Dake, a big, fluffy, blue, cuddly monster-type, in their funny dialogue and mixed words and concepts, often interrupted Pastor Tony to ask questions about what he was teaching. Pastor Tony would patiently set straight the school's fondest mascots with practical applications. Sometimes they would even make Pastor Tony laugh. Those were the best moments of all.

At the end of each chapel service Tony would ask the young audience, "Who does your heart belong to?" With a roar of noise the children would give their trained response, "Jesus!" The next question still resounds in my heart as I write. "Who else does your heart belong to?" With great enthusiasm they would yell, "Mom and Dad!" Our simple chapel was the entrance ramp to a highway for successful homes. It is based on Malachi 4:6: "He will turn the hearts of the fathers to the children, and the hearts of the children to their fathers, lest He strike the earth with a curse." Turning the hearts of the children to their earthly parents and to the Father in heaven was an easy task because they were so tender. The challenge was turning the hearts of the fathers to their own children.

Hearts must have direction and that is why the Bible uses the word "turn." Don't you wonder, "Turn from what?"

Life is a gift. Innocence is birthed with each baby's first gasp of air. Life is filled with potential. Little hearts are like sponges soaking up all that will be poured into them. Life becomes the classroom and everyone home educates to some degree. Values, prejudices, character and manners, along with a delight for learning, are taught long before any child arrives at a school campus with a backpack and lunch box in hand.

A tension can slowly develop in children at various stages,

Who Has Your Heart?

teetering between their parents and the imbalance of focusing too much time and energy on friends, games, activities and possible foolishness. Proverbs 22:15 warns that foolishness is bound up in the hearts of our children.[1]

Who will untie them?

Parents' hearts are challenged to stay focused on winning the hearts of their children and instilling godly values. To the detriment of the children, and the family's unity, there may be, instead, an overemphasis on status, career, education, money, social events and hobbies, with no regard for priorities of the heart.

In the small span of time when hearts are vulnerable and pliable, one of the consistent instructors in most homes is television. Sitcoms have degenerated into modeling homes of disorder and disrespect while training young eyes to follow their instructions, resulting in drama kings and queens in our households. Insults and sarcasm are met with canned laughter. But is anyone really laughing? This display of our evolving society and its many compromises is often permitted and even welcomed in our homes nightly as we watch it subtly communicating undesirable and harmful values. Who is winning the hearts of our children?

Keeping our heart with all diligence, coupled with turning the hearts of our children to the parents, will take determined effort. But a steady diet of entertainment enables the mind to stay in neutral.

Diligence takes energy and a game plan. "Couch potatoes" don't become champions without change. Involved parents don't become better at parenting by viewing and reading dramas of dysfunctional households. Idolizing celebrity relationships and their opinions on life must be challenged with scriptural truth and integrity. Children

Engaging the Heart

don't learn to be respectful and obedient by rolling their eyes and talking back to their parents, modeled by the young stars of television comedy. Again, I wonder who is laughing.

You can never guard a heart if you have never had it. The challenge is winning the heart. Just like seeds a gardener places in the rich soil to grow, so are our children placed in the greenhouses of our homes. Each seed is packed with potential fruit and beauty to feed multitudes, having the ability to grow and impact its world. Its miracle growth at exponential rates is a marvel. The master gardener must be diligent to let the roots grow strong before transplanting the young seedlings to larger fields and changing climates. Keeping weeds out that steal essential nutrients is necessary. Consistent watering, pruning, fertilizing and care produce a hearty plant.

Life is the gift and at the heart of every seed is the potential for increase. What tools are needed for a bountiful harvest?

Tools for guarding your heart, like a gardener's, are simple. The water is representative of God's Word. Its refreshment not only helps a child grow but also washes away the residue of the hazardous elements of the culture. The words of encouragement in training, and later coaching, fertilize the soil of the heart. Every child is in need of a master motivator in his life, like a Zig Ziglar, to say, "See You at the Top."[2] Speak life over your children and call them champions. Call them to walk above normal, reminding them what Patsy Clairmont discovered: "Normal is just a setting on your dryer."[3] Being typical is insulting when compared to the potential of their life. Teach children to search for their life's assignment and to live on purpose with purpose. Celebrate life with them and enjoy the journey together.

A watchful eye observes the weeds that are growing near the

Who Has Your Heart?

tender plants. Weeds can deceptively resemble the tender plants from which they are leaching important nutrients. It will take wisdom how to separate the two. Weeding comes through consistent conversation that challenges inappropriate behaviors and thinking processes.

Needed pruning, though temporarily painful, enables the yield to be bountiful in time. Discipline, character development and course corrections produce a life with something effective and fruitful to offer its generation.

When a young child learns to guard his heart, the developing years will be less challenging. Hearts are meant to belong to a family. Winning the heart of your child will involve times to listen, dream and grow together. Just existing together with the radio on, the headsets plugged into your child's ears, or spending hours playing computer games is a most subtle thievery. It steals time, creativity and interaction. It leaves children oblivious to needs and opportunities around them. Over-indulgence in phone calls and text messaging promotes the discourteous practices of the social culture, leaving relationships wanting around the dinner table. Properly used, however, the television and the computer are wonderful teaching tools, but open accountability is required because they allow access to an infinite number of undesirable sources of influence. Invest in conversation and tell stories about each other's lives. Learn to be an award-winning interviewer who knows the right questions to ask as you dig for gold. Use talking books, radio theater and reading aloud as a family to stimulate conversation while you grow together. Make a memory.

When a young child has turned his heart to his parents or parent, others can't steal it away easily. When our son, Connor, was playing Little League Baseball, Tony and I went to one of his tournaments.

Engaging the Heart

Lydia, our fourth-born daughter, who was nine years old at the time, was also with us. Near the ball diamond was the playground where other siblings of the team were playing, and she asked permission to go play with them. We consented but sat between the field and the playground where we could watch both Connor and Lydia.

While Lydia was playing, a young man who was fourteen approached her, saying, "Hey! You are pretty. Do you want to go on a date with me?" Unintimidated, Lydia boldly said, "No! My heart belongs to someone else." Unaccustomed to such a response, the boy left.

After the game, as we were walking to the car, Lydia told her dad what had happened earlier in the evening. Tony was upset at this young man's brashness. Visibly concerned, Tony nervously asked, "Lydia, what did you say?" She replied that she told him her heart belonged to someone else.

My husband's face must have looked shocked. Feeling dismayed that his watchful eye over his daughter had missed this unprotected moment and sobered by the set of events, he quietly asked, "Lydia, who has your heart?" Sweetly laughing, she quipped, "Daddy, it's you—you have my heart."

Chapter Two
Cup of Purity

One spring, when Anna, Lindey and Holly were younger, before Lydia and Connor were born, we spent the afternoon with friends. Our daughters liked to play together and we walked parallel roads of interest and shared similar standards. While we were visiting, my friend, Nancy, offered to show me a small china plate they had recently given to their daughter for her birthday. As I inquired more about the gift, she told me about a children's book that told the story of a young girl and her discovery of purity. It was from this book she got the idea about the china plate.

I have always been one to love application of truth, and her idea gave me one, too. When we arrived home, I asked my three daughters if they would be free to join me for a special luncheon—one at a time. They were excited about my offer and immediately asked, "Who gets to go first?" I answered, "We will go in your birth order. Anna, could you clear your social calendar for next Friday?" Smiling and showing great interest, she agreed to my invitation.

"Where will we go?" Lindey inquired. "Ah, but that is my secret!" Knowing I always have loved a surprise, the girls knew not to ask any more questions. My bluffing had worked because I yet had to plan this luncheon, but I knew it would involve teaching my young daughters about purity.

I soon made my way to the nearby Christian bookstore to find the

Engaging the Heart

children's book Nancy had mentioned. The story was a delightful one and I was in awe of its simplistic approach to such a complex message.

The day came that Anna and I were off to our surprise luncheon at a quaint restaurant that had newly opened in our town. After we ordered, I pulled the small children's book from my purse and asked Anna to read it aloud. Sipping tea and smiling, Anna began to read the story of the little girl who had learned about being set apart when she visited her elderly neighbor, Mrs. Rosey Posey.[1]

The engaging story told of a little girl with a downcast face who had come to the porch of her grandmotherly neighbor. Mrs. Rosey Posey had asked her why she was so sad. She told her the other children were able to go to the movies, but she was not allowed to go because her parents thought it was inappropriate.

With enthusiastic joy, Mrs. Rosey Posey exclaimed, "How wonderful to be loved like that!" Looking up in surprise, the little girl wondered what she could mean. Mrs. Rosey Posey said, "Would you like to come in and share some chocolate covered cherries with me I made this morning?" With her face brightening from the warm attention of her wise mentor and with her interest growing, she quickly said "yes" to the invitation.

As Mrs. Rosy Posey went to her kitchen, she passed the garbage can and pulled a used paper plate from the trash. It was smeared with leftover food. "Do you mind if we have our treats on this plate?" she asked her little guest. With wide eyes and a look of horror on her face, the little girl said, "Is that all you have?" "Oh, no! I have my everyday dishes or my fine china in the china cabinet. Which would you like?" Her young friend paused and hesitatingly said, "Your fine china would be wonderful." Cheerfully, Mrs. Rosey Posey said,

Cup of Purity

"Then the fine china it will be!"

As the two sat down for their afternoon refreshment, Mrs. Rosey Posey wisely instructed her that her life was set apart and protected like fine china. One day the King would have a special occasion to use her life but, until then, she was to be protected. Amazingly, it was the picture of a large, complex word—sanctification: being set apart.

In the tender moments and conversation that followed, I asked my firstborn daughter, "Anna, would you be willing to guard your heart and embrace purity? And would you live your life like fine china—set apart for the King's use?" She willingly said, "Yes."

I had another surprise at the end of our lunch. After our outing, Anna and I went to the finest china shop in our town. As we walked into the store of treasures, I said, "Anna, pick out any china tea cup and saucer you like to remind you of your decision to walk in purity."

I stood near the side of the rows of fine china, marveling at the different elegant patterns. Soon, my marveling turned to astonishment as I saw the prices of a place setting of china near me. Four hundred dollars and higher was the cost of the ones in the row where I stood. Immediately, I wondered how I would tell my husband he may have to mortgage something because of my simple lesson about purity. Plus, I had two more daughters to bring later.

Pondering it all, I asked myself "What price tag would you put on purity?" Reflecting on the day and the question, I determined to rest in this teaching moment and trust I would find a way to come up with the money—or get a job.

After carefully looking and examining the many patterns, Anna made her choice. It was a beautiful tea cup and saucer that matched her personality and beauty. Thankfully, we weren't buying the whole set.

We took her selection to the counter to pay for it and have it wrapped with elegant paper and a bow fit for a queen. Walking out, I quickly said, "Anna, you must not tell your sisters anything about today." The element of surprise had to be protected with each one. "You can only tell your sisters, 'We had a lovely time.'" Smiling, she agreed and we left with the treasured souvenir of an afternoon that has guided the decisions and heartfelt convictions of today.

Upon arriving home, we were met at the door that afternoon by Lindey and Holly. They persisted in asking their sister unending questions, trying to find out the details of our secret luncheon. "Your gift is beautiful! What's in it?" Anna smiled, feeling smug that she knew what they wanted to know, and replied, "I had a lovely time with Mom today." Turning from her inquisitive audience, she went up the stairs to her room to hide away her prized possession.

"Girls, there will be a day when I will call you to join me for a special breakfast and there you may bring your gift boxes. On that special day we will open the gifts together and discover the secret." Anticipation grew in the hearts of the two waiting daughters who were yet to have their outing with me.

Over the next two weeks, I took one girl each Friday to repeat the special luncheon at the same restaurant with my children's book in my purse and my memorable surprise for dessert. By now, they knew it would involve a gift of some kind but were clueless what it could be.

Amazingly, each girl picked the exact same row to walk down in the china shop. All three girls picked unique patterns of imported china that reflected their personalities. And, the manufacturer of the china was the same. Each had spent the same exact amount without knowing what the others had chosen.

A few weeks passed before I called the girls to join Tony and me at our dining room table for a very special breakfast. The table was set with our family's fine china and each girl came with their gifts in hand. Tony, too, was eager to know what lay in the beautifully wrapped boutique boxes with the large bows. Anticipation grew as we ate and talked of the special luncheons together.

Tony read aloud the children's book once more. The time came to open each gift one by one and Anna began the unveiling. We all had fun that morning as we admired each handpicked, fine china cup and saucer. I brought steeping hot tea as we sipped together from our own priceless cups.

As we listened, Tony began to read aloud the Psalm of the day. I will never forget the moment he came to a verse within the chapter that read, "Lord, You are the portion of my inheritance and my cup." It was in that moment I realized how much the Lord wanted to help us teach our children.[2]

Afterward, every New Year's Day we gave each of our daughters a full place setting to match their cup of purity. The desired intent was to furnish each with a set of twelve for their future homes. Their tables of fine china would lovingly remind them of their commitment to purity and the King who has need of them.

I am often asked when and how do you teach your children about purity. The earlier the better! My daughter Lindey says that "purity is a process and not merely a decision." Her wisdom is profound because each of us bump into things that tempt us to be impure. A magazine on a grocery stand, an inappropriate movie, unrestrained thoughts and unforgiveness are all forms of impurity and more. Even doubt is the impurity when faith is the subject at hand. The issue of purity is an area of the heart that must be guarded.

Many have tried to control impurity by outward pretense. However, Proverbs warned that you are what you think.[3] Purity is not only about sexual issues; it also reaches into every part of our lives. Deciding to embrace purity is the beginning. Understanding its value is the treasure.

Purity has often been a challenge, and when we wander off of God's course for our lives the consequences can be extreme. However, just like bleach expels all stains, the cleansing blood of Jesus washes us white as snow. This means purity can be recovered. Ask Him to restore your purity once again. "He who has clean hands and a pure heart...shall receive blessing from the Lord."[4]

There can be no sweeter story of purity recaptured than that of a close friend of one of our daughters. Though she had been attending a Christian Bible school, she still had troubling undercurrents of her life before Christ. She had been exposed to sexual abuse, promiscuous living and a former lifestyle opposite of purity. Her virginity had been taken from her at a young age, and her new life in Christ was intermingled with thoughts of the past and of forgiving herself.

One night for her birthday, we asked her to join our family at a unique restaurant where every table was round and in its own private room. After our dinner and celebrating her life, we gave her a specially wrapped gift box. Inside the wrapping was her own fine china cup and saucer. She began to cry as we reminded her that

CUP OF PURITY

old things are passed away and she is new because of the love and forgiveness of the King of her heart.

She keeps her cup of purity on her bedside table. Her life now impacts others, even in other nations, as she serves abused young girls with a heart that is pure. The Redeemer has become her portion and continues to fill her cup of purity with Himself.

Chapter Three
The Blessing

The year of the blessing is a special event for our family. It has always been when our five children, Anna, Lindey, Holly, Lydia and Connor have reached the bridge that begins to cross over the gap between childhood and adulthood. Our culture labels this passage as the teenage years. It is in these years that winning their hearts for the cause of Christ is essential. If ever the blessing is needed it is when our children are learning to apply all they have been trained in up to this moment. In the middle of peer pressure, increased studies, friends and learning to think independently, God's favor is welcomed.

It is during this year we designate times to call or meet with people in our lives who have impacted us and care about our family. Usually, there is a special event where the grandparents and family members, along with spiritual leaders, come. We place the twelve-year-old child in the center of the gathering and begin speaking words of encouragement and inspiration to them. This special moment validates how much their life is valued.

Often there are handpicked verses of encouragement and direction that are read. Many have words of wisdom as they begin telling the honored daughter or son of the gift they see in them. Each one comes sharing a blessing of a memory or a wish for them as we celebrate their life. After the sharing, we pray over the celebrated twelve-year-old and speak the blessing found in Numbers 6:24-26:

The Blessing

"May the Lord bless you and keep you. May His face shine upon you and be gracious to you. May the Lord lift up His countenance upon you and give you peace." The blessing paves the entrance for a season that to most is troubling and unclear.

We take the entire year to set it apart for the blessing because some of these friends and special leaders are from all over the nation, and even the world. I have watched in amazement as He has orchestrated trips for us to visit these key people or for them to come to us. If we had made a guest list, they would have been the very names we would have included.

Over the years, God has brought special relationships into our lives that have fundamentally impacted our home and family. Such is the case when we met our dear friends and lifelong mentors, Bill and Dorothy Jean Ligon. These friends have now become family as we have learned from them the extraordinary power of the blessing.

Tony and I were engaged when we first met the Ligons, and they transformed our hearts as we learned about the Father's Blessing,[1] as they entitled it. With every season, that message has grown in our hearts and lives. In fact, one church in Dallas always referred to us as the "blessing family." Speaking the blessing became more than just a teaching; it became our lifestyle.

The blessing in the book of Numbers is referred to as the priestly blessing because the Lord instructed the priests to pray it over the children of Israel. The promise is that the name of God will be invoked over them like an umbrella of protection and favor. It is like having a baseball cap of your favorite team. You demonstrate to a watching world that this team is your choice and its branding is your covering.

Engaging the Heart

Having the name of God over us is greater than that of any champion sports team who has some victories and some losses. God never fails. He is the Great "I Am" who is the answer to all you ask. His name is above all other names and His blessings are "exceedingly, abundantly, above all you could think, imagine or dream," as we are told in Ephesians 3:20.

Over the years, we have watched as the Ligons modeled the importance of the spoken blessing in the home. Also, we have admired their congregation who, from the youngest to the oldest, speak the blessing to others.

The lifestyle of embracing the blessing is the remedy for insult and curses. 1 Peter 3:9 states that we are not to return evil for evil, or insult for insult, but instead, speak the blessing. The blessing defuses the conflicts of life and wishes good on both your friends and your enemies. The end of that passage enlightens us to see that "we are called to inherit a blessing." God can't help but continually bless His own, and we imitate His intent when we speak the blessing over others.

Since the early days of our marriage and beginning our family, Tony has been diligent to speak the blessing over his household. Our children learned its importance and, as an overflow of his practices, learned to quote the words, too. I can remember when, at the age of eighteen months, our son, Connor, would stand inside his crib while his daddy spoke the blessing over him at night. Tony's nightly regimen consisted of multiple verses that came alive as he would speak them over his children. Even at Connor's young age, he would remain standing in his crib until his Dad completed the verses of blessings by memory. On cue, Connor would lay his head down on his pillow, knowing the day was over.

The Blessing

Now the practice has continued as our married children do the same with their children. I remember when our first grandson was being trained with the blessing. He knew it was bedtime when his mommy or daddy would speak the verses from the book of Numbers. He would quiet himself by placing his thumb in his mouth as they climbed the steps to his bedroom. Upon approaching his crib, the blanket of blessing enveloped a man of God in the making.

One evening when we lived in Illinois, Tony and Anna, three years old at the time, went to a church production at Christmas. As they were both taking their winter coats off, Tony began to speak the blessing over Anna while he hung up her coat. In the middle, Tony started to cough. While he was temporarily interrupted, Anna finished the verse perfectly. Tony was amazed since she had only heard the passage and we had never worked with her to memorize it.

Every morning when my husband would take the children to school, their routine involved the blessing being spoken over them. It was more than words; it had become a way of life and part of our conversation. One particular day, our daughters were going to leave with friends. Once on the front porch, they turned back quickly and yelled, "Hey, we're leaving. Aren't you going to say the blessing over us?"

The spoken blessing is not angelic fairy dust or a temporary fix to life's complexities. It is the keen awareness that life apart from His blessing is mere survival. We must see our destiny and purpose in the framework of God's bigger picture.

As the children grew and new responsibilities and privileges were given to them, they often had to make choices and ask permission. I would ask, "Do you want my permission or my blessing?" Both were potentially available, but only one carried the favor and protection of our authority as their parents.

We have seen broken hearts in relationships mended with the spoken blessing. Forgiveness is jarred loose when the blessing is spoken over the ones who have offended them. The blessing sets your course for more of Him. Speaking the blessing to others is always a timely and appreciated gift.

The blessing is a heart tenderizer. Seeds of blessings produce bumper harvests of favor and kindness. Insults tear down and evil destroys, but the blessing encourages and models Christ. Even in the time of Jesus, there was a day among the crowds that tells of a specific group of children who had come to the side of the Master. The disciples quickly discouraged their coming and told them, "Don't bother Jesus."[2]

Jesus quickly told the disciples to let them come. The Bible says they came and sat on his lap and He laid His hands on them. I imagine that He may have spoken the well-known blessing of Numbers 6:24-26 as He embraced these little ones. His attending disciples saw the children as an interruption and inconvenience, but the loving Rabbi saw them as the leaders of tomorrow and seized the moment. When was the last time you spoke the blessing over your children?

In our wedding, in the middle of the ceremony, we had our fathers pray over us and pronounce the blessing. Our future marital bliss needed more than just our human love and effort. When our firstborn daughter lay dying after her birth with seven critical complications, we began to speak the blessing over her, praying to the Great Physician to show us His mercy. The doctors had indicated it was hopeless and had begun to write her death certificate. The blessing generated life and invited His hand of intervention. The meaning

The Blessing

of Anna's name is "gracious gift." She says it reminds her to be gracious to others because God has been gracious to her. Spoken blessings make a difference in hopeless circumstances. They are life-giving.

In the car on the way to various events, big or small, Tony will begin from the driveway speaking the blessing over his family and adding multiple verses that focus us on the Lord's name and purpose. Whether they are recitals, Little League ball games, dinners, weddings, funerals or life in between, the blessing is always welcomed. Graduations, birthdays, and upon departing someone's home, the blessing is appropriate.

Our family was invited to Zig Ziglar's 80th birthday extravaganza at the Gaylord in Dallas, Texas. After the celebration and inspiring program of honor, Mr. Ziglar sat at the edge of the stage for guests to come by and speak to him. The line was exhaustingly long and he had become visibly tired. Our family waited toward the end of the line. When we approached him, he was kind and remembered who we were. We said, "Mr. Ziglar we want to bless you." As we began in unison to speak the blessing, He stood up, suddenly energized, popped a mint in his mouth and smiling, warmly thanked us with hugs as he received his blessing. From store managers, doctors, teachers, families to coaches, the blessing fits all groups and personalities.

There could be nothing more important than children learning to value and respect the blessing and learning to give it away, too. One evening when I was sitting on the stage with the faculty at Christ For The Nations in Dallas, Connor, five years old at the time, came up after the meeting to stand with me. I had introduced our son to several when the preacher of all preachers stepped over to greet me. "John, I would like you to meet the next generation of preachers.

Engaging the Heart

This is our son, Connor." John bent down to shake his hand and enthusiastically encouraged him in his upcoming role. Looking my son's way, I suggested Connor speak the blessing to this seasoned leader who is a favorite on campus with his homiletics classes.

Connor looked him in the eyes and with the boldness of a grown man, said, "May the Lord bless you and keep you and the Lord make His face to shine upon you and be gracious to you. May the Lord lift up His countenance upon you and give you peace." John, now crying, bent down to hug Connor and thanked him for the best sermon he had ever heard.

This past spring when we were speaking in the Georgia Golden Coast, we were invited to the home of the Ligons. During dinner it dawned on me we were days away from our last child's twelfth birthday. Our visit suddenly seemed like a divine appointment on God's calendar. He now had arranged for all of our five children to be with the one who first taught us to bless. As Connor knelt in front of this beloved, seasoned man of God, I felt the tears fall softly on my cheeks. Over thirty years had passed since we first heard about the Father's blessing. Amazingly, Bill had been involved with each of our children's twelfth year spoken blessing. How rich our lives have been to know this truth.

Afterwards, Connor and Bill engaged in an arm wrestling match, instigated by Bill, seventy-seven years of age at the time. Through tears of laughter now, I watched the two men lie on their stomachs on the floor to arm wrestle. The budding strength of our son was challenged by a man in his seventies who had the strength of a young warrior. His lifetime of giving blessings and a lifestyle of blessing others reminded me that the strong bless.

With red faces, Connor surfaced first as the winner. However, on

The Blessing

the way home later, Connor said, "He let me win tonight."

The laying on of hands had come through kneeling and then warring. The blessing prepares you for both as we humbly walk before our God and bless others.

The next day brought an honor that almost felt awkward. The Ligons asked us to meet them at their son's law firm, who is also a judge. They arranged to have their son's family there to receive the blessing from us. In the conference room, one by one the five young grandchildren came to stand before us for their portion of the blessing. I realized then the message of the blessing was generational.

The most sobering of all twelfth-year blessings came with our fourth-born daughter, Lydia. We were in Dallas the night before her actual birthday, celebrating with our family and my parents at our favorite restaurant. My husband spotted our dear friend and fellow minister from Zimbabwe who was in Dallas to speak for a conference. After we greeted him, we asked more about the conference the next evening. "Tomorrow is our daughter's birthday and it is good we have celebrated tonight so we can attend." Then I quickly asked, "Would you prayerfully consider speaking the blessing over Lydia when we meet again?" Without hesitation, he replied, "It would be my honor."

We arrived early at the church where the conference was being held. The Pastor ushered us to his office where we could pray. Within minutes, the man of God from Africa came into the room with five others. He asked if his ministry board could pray over our daughter, too. They also had come to our city to participate in the conference.

I stepped back as the men surrounded Lydia and watched as they prayed. Each spoke powerful words with a prophetic edge. In

Engaging the Heart

astonishment, I looked closely at the men who were praying. The regions of Europe, South America, the British Isles, Africa and America were represented by these Christian ambassadors. This had not been by chance. Thinking of our daughter's love for evangelism, I remembered the origin of her given name. Her full name, Lydia Ellison, represented evangelists of long ago.

Lydia in the scriptures used her business wealth, as a seller of purple, to help fund the evangelistic crusades of the apostle Paul. She was the first European convert to Christianity.

Ellison was the name of my great-grandfather. He, too, was the first of his family to give his life to Christ. As a farmer, he witnessed in rural communities, often in their one-room school buildings. His life, however, was shortened due to illness. It is said that on his death bed he led his neighbors to Christ.

Only time will tell regarding the call and life-assignment for our daughter, Lydia. Clearly, God had brought the nations to bless her on the very day she turned twelve. God had orchestrated this divine, global appointment for a day yet to be fulfilled.

The blessing is far-reaching, touching generations and many regions of the world. May our children and our children's children desire the blessing of the Lord. May they choose His blessing over mere permission. May they open their hearts to inherit all of His blessings. May they know how to bless others.

Chapter Four
Sleeping Beauty

While still living with my parents as a twenty-year-old, I was sitting on the edge of my bed late one night. I was crying as my mother tried to comfort me. "Mom, I am lonely and confused. I want to be married and have a family." She assured me, "Gail, you know God has someone special for you." "Then where is he?!" I sobbed. Immediately, the phone next to my bed rang. I quickly wiped my tears; after all, it might be for me!

It took three rings for me to clear my voice. Reaching for the phone before answering it, I quipped, "Mom! Maybe this will be my man of God." There was a crackling sound on the line. Suspecting it was a long-distance call with a poor connection, I wondered who it could be. I was shocked to hear, "Hello! This is Tony McWilliams."

With the phone receiver in one hand and my other hand pointing to the phone for my watching Mom to share in this bizarre timing of events, I stuttered loudly, "Uh…Tony McWilliams!"

I had only met Tony a few weeks earlier. He and some other young men were working on a college campus in Illinois a few miles from our house. He had been traveling with a ministry that was part business and part evangelism. He sold stationery, invitations and letterheads to fraternities and sororities while leaving gospel tracts and literature to witness to students. In the summer months they interned at a Christian center. It is in this setting my husband learned

Engaging the Heart

to develop his gift for teaching God's word and loving His ways.

Tony's call that night makes me smile as I think back to the timing of it all. In my temporary meltdown over my desire to be married, God had a plan. I was previously thinking I might have to get ready to enter a monastery and be a nun at the ripe old age of twenty. How very young that seems now.

Tony and I had a unique dating relationship. Our courtship was different because we both were traveling the United States in separate ministries. We, nonetheless, found time to talk on the phone, write love letters and see each other as often as we could. Though there was not a long list of previous suitors, we had dated others before we met. These painful, and sometimes awkward, dating relationships left us wanting something different for our own children.

It is interesting to me that some parents have rejected the idea of protecting their sons and daughters by allowing unrestrained social dating. I often hear, "Hey! We turned out all right. Just let them have fun." Surely, there is a more excellent way than repeating the mistakes of the previous generation. A father has the best vantage point for knowing a young man's motives and passions. Passively hoping everything will be fine is naïve. Mothers have the advantage of training their sons how a lady would like to be treated while encouraging her daughter to respect herself and others. To me, the real key is constant communication—starting as early as possible.

During the pastoring years, my husband was leading a men's prayer breakfast in our church. While food was being prepared, the discussion of purity and dating started with Tony and one of the men in attendance. This man was a father of a teenage daughter. Perplexed by the growing awareness of purity issues, he admitted to the difficulty of relating to its importance. Questioning, he asked,

Sleeping Beauty

"What's the big deal anyway?" Overhearing the discussion, another man joined the conversation, interjecting a thought-provoking question. Challenging the father's bewilderment, he asked, "Think about it. What kind of thoughts were going through your head when you were seventeen years old?" The man deliberately thought for a few precious seconds then responded, "I'll kill him! I'll kill him!" During that important light-bulb moment the fathers enjoyed a laugh together.

Parents need to be honest with themselves as they remember back to the tensions of growing adolescence. If we cannot relate with our children, who will? Keep the principles of purity and their benefits constantly before your children's eyes and do what you can to paint the picture of life with no regrets. Let them know you are for them. There can be no greater joy than to see them succeed. As you remember your youthful inclinations and temptations, you can never start too early helping your child navigate through relationships.

I remember when Connor was in kindergarten and his innocent attraction to a beautiful young girl. She was, by far, the prettiest girl in his class, and he had noticed. One day after school, he was frustrated as he told me what had happened that afternoon. She was walking down the sidewalk with her arms filled with books for "Show and Tell." Connor sweetly said, "May I carry your books for you?" To which she rudely responded, "No!" After she had walked a few steps away from him, Connor raised his voice for her to hear and said, "My mom says to treat every woman like a queen." She abruptly stopped and waited for Connor to catch up with her. Without saying a word, she handed him her books. And the two of them walked on to class.

All of our parents walked in the light they had and most families did a good job. However, I hope more light has been given to my generation, believing it will be increased even more in the next.

Fears of being called "old fashioned" or "a prude" are often excuses for saying, "I don't want to put forth the effort to make it safer for my children." Others are clueless where to begin. In many cases, to think of doing it differently might disclose our own failures and wrong choices. Those private talks with our children may include discretely revealing some of our own failures as we humbly ask our children to forgive us for compromises that are linked to struggles they now face. Being authentic will win the hearts of our young people in households worldwide. It could also open the door for them to tell us their temptations before it is too late. Communication and praying together will fuse our hearts to work for each other's success.

Is it only in fairy tales a prince with charm finally appears and his sleeping beauty awakens to love that is everlasting? The tragic ballads of love-gone-wrong and hearts broken cause you to wonder if too many frogs have been kissed in hopes of discovering a happy ending. The modern dating experiment resembles people who casually leap from one relationship to another. How do you guard your heart in the dating season?

In an attempt to help our girls navigate through youthful attractions and puppy love, we desired to show our commitment to our daughters. At the age of thirteen our girls were given special rings. Long before it was the fad to wear jewelry as a symbol of embracing purity and courtship, we searched for something significant to express our love and commitment to them. Purity has always been about more than just a piece of jewelry. The heart is at stake.

Upon their turning thirteen, Tony went with each daughter to shop

Sleeping Beauty

for rings. Several top choices were made, with the agreement he would go back and pick the one he thought might please his young princess the most.

The ring symbolized several things. The first was the determined commitment to be a prayer covering for them in everything, including praying for their man of God to come in God's timing. The other meanings of the ring stated our daughters would be respected as they communicated what they desired in a future mate. The girls always knew it was not a binding ring of isolation, betrothal or denial. They knew they had veto power over anyone who came knocking at our door. We made a commitment to work together as a team.

During the teen years, our family went to a nearby town to minister. We stayed with a family with two sons that became dear friends and we all enjoyed being together. One of their boys and one of our daughters were close in age and enjoyed each other's company. Nothing happened between them and the two were never alone, yet they often exchanged glances across the room.

On one occasion when we had left our friends and were traveling home from the small Midwest town, I asked our young ladies, "Did we leave anyone's heart behind? Is your heart safely here?" A resounding reply came from the trio of sisters in the back seat, "Yes, Mom!"

We have always talked about everything, especially heart issues and accountability, giving them assurance that no one is an old maid at fifteen. True love and romance, indeed, can wait.

Lindey's ring best symbolized our family's commitment. It was three golden strands that were intertwined together. We said one strand was for Lindey's heart, the other for our commitment to help protect her, and the other for Jesus' enduring love. There is a verse in Ecclesiastes that states, "A three-fold cord is not easily broken."[1]

Lydia's ring is a silver knot that symbolizes being tied to her parents' hearts and to God's principles. One day her ring will be exchanged for the ring of her husband who will pledge his heart to her.

We know with each of our children their stories of discovering a mate will be different and memorable. It will be principles that will anchor them in the middle of the diversity of their individual lives.

All of us love romantic classics we have shared together. We read aloud novels like *The Secret Garden* and *Little Women* and have watched *Anne of Green Gables* and *Pride and Prejudice*. Always talking together, we would discuss the characters and their actions.

Are there benefits to conducting yourself differently from the typical dating standard where two people isolate themselves from the rest of the world? With the interest and active involvement of parents, young people, who are not old enough to even consider marriage anyway, can develop genuine friendships, including those with the opposite sex. Friendships can develop when your heart is intact and you are not desperately looking for someone to be with or for a hand to hold. The focus is to engage in the freedom singleness brings. It takes a secure heart to stand alone and respond to life based on principles and not just follow the crowd.

A helpful tool I used with the girls was to role play. Many times we would be in situations with eligible young men who may be looking for new fair maidens to impress. I would think of scenarios that would prepare them for any possible situation. I thought if they could unemotionally choose ahead of time the wisdom needed for that moment, then a real life event would only be a rerun; for they had already been there.

Most do not realize that the concept of dating is a relatively new idea. It has become increasingly accepted in the last 100 years as the norm. Some love it and embrace it like a timeshare plan—a new place and memory for every changing season. The difference between one person's definition of dating and someone else's is vast. You give your heart to one and then become bored or uninterested and move on to another. Is dating practice for divorce?

Courtship is a word used to describe a method of developing relationships with the opposite sex while having extensive involvement from parents or mentors. Guarded hearts within group activities leave room for safe and honest discovery until the appropriate time of giving one's heart fully in marriage. Room is made and time allowed for character qualities to be displayed. Genuine friendships are developed creating a contrast to the modern dating practices that focus mainly on physical attraction and affection.

In some circles, in an effort to make dating seem more honorable, the word courtship has replaced the word dating, but the fruit of it is often the same. Courtship is not being isolated and your parents micro-managing your social calendar. Instead, courtship creates freedom to live your life with a heart that is unentangled, a conscience that is clear and a morality that is without compromise. I believe the core issue is guarding the heart.

One night while at dinner with another family, we were discussing the heart of a single young lady. The phrase of the evening was to be "asleep in Christ." If a young single woman was asleep it did not mean she had to miss out on life and be comatose. Quite to the contrary, it described a season where no special person of interest distracted her as she was broadening her skills, education, interests and just loving life. In this state she could be focused as she waited for the day her prince would arrive for her hand. Though the concept may seem a bit like a fairy tale, the posture is more peaceful than anxiously looking at every male who walks in the door and asking, "Is he the one?"

We broke out in hilarious laughter when one of our friend's oldest daughter said, "I don't mind being asleep in Christ, but can I keep one eye open?"

I have talked with many who are afraid to involve the Lord in picking out their life partner. After all, they reason, they are the one who has to live with the person. They try to justify that they need to look around and try some out first. In reality, they don't even know fully what they want. They want to be solely involved in the selection process for fear of marrying a dud. What if substance guided our decisions more than fear? A sleeping beauty is not in denial about her emotions, but trusts. Grace covers her and she is unmoved by the world spinning around her. Her heart is at peace.

You can rest, knowing the Lover of your soul will orchestrate events and gatherings that will open your eyes. Just remember to do as my dad warned me one evening: "Gail, you can have whatever you want, but you must choose wisely."

When we lived in Central Illinois, I frequently asked my daughters, "Do you want the best this county can offer, or do you want the best in the world God has for you?" Best is relative when focused only on your small community. His lineup may be more appealing. His eyes see it all. You can rest in the One who knows you better than you know yourself. Let him hold your heart as you embrace these days of singleness. Maximize the potential of your increased beauty and ability. Soon, someone special, just for you, will awaken you

Chapter Five
Secret Garden

One Spring when our youngest children were in diapers and our three oldest daughters were pre-teens, we traveled to Pennsylvania to stay with friends. They had three lovely, refined daughters who were older than our girls. Their family served as a living version of our dream pattern for the home. Their seasoned elegance and polished beauty were vast contrasts to our wet clay pottery that was still in process.

Their home was excellent and their minds and gifts brilliant. One afternoon, their three daughters and lovely mother took our family on a memorable sightseeing tour in historic Philadelphia near the Liberty Bell.

In this grand historic setting we stopped to have a picnic lunch in the beautiful gardens of Liberty Park. Nestled away from the sounds of the city and all its noise, we sat on park benches and talked about issues of the heart. The setting was perfect for the discussion that followed.

I had asked them over lunch in that small scenic garden to share with us about dating, courtship and managing the heart. Rebekah, the mother, said, "Our daughters' hearts are like a garden, mentioned in the Song of Solomon.[1] The fresh fountains, fruit-bearing plants and sweet fragrances reflect their lives, filled with potential and new buds." She continued, "The garden will need some attention to develop into its full beauty: watering, weeding, pruning and a

Engaging the Heart

watchful eye." "Rebekah," I asked, "Where do you see the father in this garden." With a soft voice and birds singing nearby, she answered, "He stands at the gate of the garden."

She went on to tell of his responsibility to insure the garden is not interrupted by unwelcomed visitors who may try to steal the fruit and joy of a daughter before it has time to blossom and become ripe. She wisely pointed out that even a simple pebble could impede the growth of a seedling. The sunshine is essential for growth and she warned that friends of any kind or gender must, by necessity, bring light to the garden and not darkness. Ideally, the father is to actively engage with the garden's growth and well-being while securing the safety of his secret garden — the heart of his daughter.

Our older daughters' attention was captured as much as mine while Rebekah shared that afternoon. I pondered aloud, "A garden of such beauty will have admirers. What will you do with them?" Rebekah warned that no admirer had the right to steal away the fruit before it was time. Some admirers may come too early and will need to return in a later season. "The gatekeeper will need wisdom," she remarked.

Rebekah continued, "Interestingly, the passage ends by telling of the winds from the north and south that will come, yet her fragrance will be enjoyed by all." Wondering the meaning of this last part of the scripture in Song of Solomon, I asked, "What do the winds represent in your picturesque garden?" Rebekah thought for a moment and said, "The north winds represent the cold harsh winds of adversity, while the south winds represent the pleasurable times." She continued by saying, "In both seasons, a heart should be focused on the Master Gardener. He is the One who, in time, will bring forth the fruit whose taste will be pleasant to all."

SECRET GARDEN

Satisfied and reflecting, I sat back, suddenly aware of the skyscrapers surrounding this quaint setting. I compared them with the modern culture that blocks the full potential of the sun's rays on our family gardens. The delicate placement of the garden in Liberty Park in the middle of a bustling world with concrete fixtures was the portrait of our changing times. It also reflects the modern dating methods we have embraced as "normal" and "typical." How will we find a path to such a garden when it is littered with the criticisms of being less modern and seemingly old-fashioned?

I wonder who will guard the hearts of our young. Will there be fathers at the gates who will commit to guard and protect? Will young hearts wait for love to mature while growing in the secret garden?

As I reflect back on that afternoon in Philadelphia near the Liberty landmark of history, I see how the background was profound on every level. Just down the pathway is Independence Hall. The Liberty Bell had been brought there originally to celebrate our freedom and to remember the declaration of our nation's independence.

When the bell was first brought to Philadelphia, it had a hairline flaw. After some time, the gap was widened and attempts were made to file the two sides of the growing crack. Shortly afterwards, the gap became a large compound fracture, making the bell tragically soundless.

The last ring from this bell of liberty was heard in 1846. The Philadelphia Public Ledger reads in its February 26, 1846 publication:

"The old Independence Bell rang its last clear note on Monday last in honor of the birthday of Washington and now hangs in the great city steeple irreparably cracked and dumb. It had been cracked before but was set in order of that day by having the edges of the fracture filed so as not to vibrate against each other ... It gave out clear notes and loud, and appeared to be in excellent condition until noon, when it received a sort of compound fracture in a zigzag direction through one of its sides which put it completely out of tune and left it a mere wreck of what it was."

When the article of the Ledger reported the damaged Liberty Bell in the 1800's, the last remark alarms me with the similarities of our homes today—"left it a mere wreck of what it was." Many homes, marriages and families are a "mere wreck" of what they once were. The "zigzag" effects of shifting standards and a culture despising the Judeo-Christian principles have left our society in a state of disrepair. Provocative television programs, sensual movies, inoculation to sin, and perversion with mounting sexual assaults have broken our moral encasement. Disposable marriages, aborted children, rising sodomy and faltering faith in Jesus Christ has widened the breech. Increased divorces, neglected children and abandoned dreams heighten our cries, but no one hears the sound.

Our homes have become "independent halls." We live in independence of God and His wisdom, and purity and virtue are regarded as optional.

Only the Great Redeemer has the ability and desire to make the shattered pieces whole once more. Lord, sing over us with Your song of love as we turn our hearts back to You. Repair what has been damaged and restore us once again.

Chapter Six
The Impostor

What if, in the search for authentic love, you give your heart to an impostor?

It was getting late in the afternoon by the time Jan arrived home from her teaching job. Her two young boys followed her into the house that was secluded in the wooded plains near the river bank. Looking at the clock, noticing it was already half past four, she wondered where her husband could be. Normally, he was the first one home.

She began quieting her anxieties by thinking about what she would prepare for dinner that evening. Scurrying around the kitchen, she wondered aloud, "Where could he be?" Their mutual agreement was to notify each other if they were ever going to be late. However, he hadn't called.

The last time she had seen her husband was that morning when they kissed goodbye. He told her he was leaving early to get the radiator fixed on his truck before going on to work. In spite of some injuries he had sustained on his job, he continued to work for the same company. Her husband had recently received a medical settlement for his extended months of pain and altered work assignments. Depression had plagued him for the past several months, and the whole family had been on pins and needles during these times of his dealing with pain.

Engaging the Heart

Concerned, Jan went to look in her husband's closet to see if anything was missing, but all was normal and in place. The fears of patterns of the past now crowded her mind as she tried to suppress the memories of earlier days in their marriage. Formerly, on occasion, he would be gone from their home for days, at random times and with no explanation or excuses; however, he would eventually come home. Those days seemed like a distant past, until now. It had been three years since it had last happened. Their family had grown close together and was involved in our church and Christian school. Jan's husband was a kind, southern gentleman who was liked by everyone. No one knew of his history.

Jan remembered all too well the last time he had disappeared. It was for three months. Though he never drank at home, he had left for the Gulf on a drinking binge without anyone knowing his whereabouts until much later. Their household funds were spent on this escapade, and even his wedding ring was missing when he returned. He seemed to have lost memory of what he had done, and he never divulged the secrets of where he had gone.

Jan's first experience of being abandoned by her husband was during their honeymoon. In the middle of their first night together, he left her, with no word or a note. Frantic and afraid, Jan went back to her parents. It was three days before her new groom returned to his abandoned bride.

Over a ten-year span Jan had learned to set her heart on the Lord. She delighted in her sons and their home. Her forgiving ways and steadfast love anchored their family. God had caused her to grow in faith and her enthusiastic joy was unwavering through it all. However, at this moment, fear gripped her heart as she wondered why her husband was late tonight.

The Impostor

Jan picked up the phone to call her husband's supervisor to ask when her husband had left work. The supervisor confirmed Jan's deepest fear. "He did not come to work today." Her heart told her he was gone.

Days earlier, the settlement money had come and their joy had been increasing as they dreamed of new beginnings and a new home of their own. They had been looking excitedly for property. Dreams now threatened to become nightmares as this deserted family began to search for their husband and beloved father—and for answers.

Jan made a second call. This one was to me. "Gail, I have reason to believe my husband is missing. Would you pray?"

Jan and her family were always willing to do anything for anyone. Through the years, God had brought healing to their home. Tony and I had seen Jan's husband the night before when he found us at the city mall where churches were being showcased in a community bazaar. He came with a smile on his face and handed Tony a tithe check from the settlement he had just received. He told us we were loved, and his offering to the church was one he gave with joy. How could things have changed in less than twenty-four hours?

His unexplained disappearance left the three with shattered hearts and confusion. "Lord, we place our trust in You," was Jan's cry. She stood firm in her strength and had complete trust in Him. She exchanged her present abandonment for being enfolded in the arms of a loving Savior who had promised never to leave or forsake her.[1]

The search for the missing husband and father was in vain. No calls came, except for the call from the mechanic the following day saying, "Your husband left his thermos at my radiator shop. I just thought you might want to know." There were no other calls until nearly four months later.

The voice on the other end of the line was of a young woman. She began by stating her full name, announcing, "I have reason to believe you are my mother-in-law. Your husband is my husband's father." Startled, Jan listened as the caller went on. "Your husband left my husband's mother when she was pregnant. I am calling because my husband has a rare illness and we are trying to get information from his birth father. "Can you help me?"

Shocked by the possibility, Jan asked her questions that would clarify if she had the right number. The facts and stories were overwhelming, and she knew the caller was legitimate. Jan began to tell her the man she was looking for had disappeared from their lives, too. Jan's husband was an impostor. In fact, he was not her husband at all.

Jan's missing husband had been spending years living with tales of secrets and lies along the way. He had never dissolved any of his previous marriages, and it was unclear how many that could be. The woman on the phone asked if she could have permission to continue the search. Jan agreed and asked if she would let her know what she found out.

Three years passed before Jan and her sons had evidence of where her husband and their father had gone. He was living in another state, had remarried, and had yet another family. This impostor father and husband had unsuspecting households in many states that had been left behind with shattered hearts. Jan was one of many who had opened her heart to an impostor.

One of our favorite old classic movies is the original version of *Pride and Prejudice*. The story is about a man who had five unmarried

The Impostor

daughters. The father, Mr. Bennett, is calm and loving, in contrast to his wife who is a clamorous, nervous mother who wants nothing but the best for herself and husbands for her daughters, preferably wealthy ones. A heart with integrity is not on the top of her list.

Some of the characters that take the center stage of this classic story are two men. One is cautious and sometimes curt, but ever watchful. The other is personable and makes good friends quickly with the young sisters. Though, at first glance he may seem to be the nicer fellow, he is, instead, an impostor with skeletons in his closet and life behaviors he has managed to cover up.

His name is Wickham and, in time, his past is revealed. The watchful man, Mr. Darcy, knows his past well but does not unveil this man publicly. Contrarily, Wickham immediately works to turn the interest and heart of the Bennett daughter, Lizzie, from Mr. Darcy. By telling her lies, he soon prejudices her from making friends with Mr. Darcy, who, in reality, is a man of noble character and principle.

The scheme might have worked except for a devastating crisis to Lizzie's family. Her young sister, Lydia, leaves with Wickham and marries him. Lydia is one who lacks maturity and scruples. She seeks only to marry quickly and has no understanding of guarding her heart. Trapped, Wickham and the young Lydia become entangled with a world of lies, cover-ups, and superficial love. Their relationship brings shame to Lizzie Bennett and her family. The cautious and watching Mr. Darcy knows too well of Wickham's past. He diligently works to help rectify the hidden trails of corruption and losses because of his respect and growing fondness of the Bennett household and their second-born daughter, Lizzie.

Though there is much more to this classic novel by Jane Austin,

Engaging the Heart

our family always anticipates the time in the movie when Mr. Darcy is revealed as a man of honor. Through many circumstances, Lizzie's eyes are opened to see his value and valor. No matter how many times we all have seen this story, our hearts love the moment of truth—discovered when two noble hearts find genuine love.

Consequently, "Wickham" has always been a code word in our home as we watch the character, or lack of it, in young men we have met over the years. An impostor by definition is a person who tries to be someone other than himself. His actions are an attempt to gain what he cannot achieve on his own. The mask he wears disguises what His own character cannot obtain. An impostor imposes himself on someone else for personal gain, having no regard for another life.

Such was the case when a young "Wickham" entered our lives. One evening, a young single pastor came to our home for dinner to spend the evening with our family. He had been attending a conference and asked if he could come to our house instead of attending one of the night sessions. We had ministered in his church several times.

When the doorbell rang that night, I answered the door. The girls were in the kitchen finishing the last details of our dinner preparations, and Tony had not yet arrived.

I was warm to him but felt a hesitation to invite him into the inner coziness of our home at first. Thinking it strange at the time, I followed my heart's instincts and asked him to sit and talk with me in the formal living room for a moment. Though we had been to his church in another town, I did not really know him as a man outside the pulpit.

I asked him questions about his life and family. His answers were

The Impostor

polished and flawless. Inquiring more, I asked what caused him to have a heart for the ministry and serving the Lord. Once more he had the right answers. We talked on about mutual friends and I kept interviewing him with questions he seemed to enjoy. They all made him look very good. Soon, his countenance changed when I asked the next question.

Calling him by name, I asked, "What is the intent of your heart?" Pausing, he cleared his throat and searched for unrehearsed answers. I then asked, "What challenges do you face as a single man who pastors?" Once more, thinking while adjusting his mask, he soon told me of a current relationship with a young lady in his congregation that concerned others around him. He even asked if I would write her and help mentor this young lady who was also new in her faith.

At dinner that evening our guest was surrounded by a happy family with diverse conversations. Later, everyone joined in with tennis and volleyball, keeping our daughters in a safe setting that night. He was overly attentive to our three older daughters.

This same young pastor was a master impostor. He had used his charm and personality to help cover up the intent of his heart. Tragically, months later, he was arrested and sent to prison after being charged with over sixty sexual assaults in the small communities and churches where he served. Many of the young teenage girls of the church, along with some married women, opened their hearts to this impostor who faced them in the congregation each and every Sunday. I could not help but wonder if our daughters were on his potential list, too.

Guarding your heart is proactive and the right questions can unlock hidden motivations. Sometimes, though, we rush relationships without taking time to watch the fruit of another life. Our haste to be loved at all costs diminishes our ability to discern.

What would cause someone to embrace a fraud when their true heart's desire is authentic love?

Couples in love overlook warning signs or potential flaws and excuse questionable conduct because they fear losing what they have already invested in the relationship. The fear of not being loved causes many to be vulnerable. Not all things that shine are gold. Fool's gold looks the same as real until you take a closer look.

Not all impostors are so flagrant. People who marry to disguise their lust become easily bored with marriage. Some are subtle and their own hearts lie to them. Tony and I know several who married and had children to cover their secret nightlife of homosexual activity. When the men were with Christians and focused on renewing their minds with the Word of God, they flourished. However, wrong friends and influences quickly enabled them to go back to their former lives—secretly.

Such was the case with two precious families. One family had seemed happily married with three children. They had determined to spend their lives helping others in a ministry. Soon, the demand for the husband's teaching ministry opened new doors around the country and he traveled without his family most of the time. In that setting it became easy to slide back into a lifestyle that eventually ended his marriage and alienated his children, while compromising his own health. Was he always an impostor trying to cover his desires and only used his family as a storefront cover-up? What about their hearts that broke when they discovered the truth? The man's love for them could not match the driving love for his own desires.

Tony and I talked with parents who were devastated over a

The Impostor

situation involving their daughter concerning the pregnancy of her fourth child. She and her husband worked alongside her parents who were pastors in a small community. Her husband had a leadership role in the church.

It was one unforgettable afternoon that she was forced to identify her impostor, much to her shocked surprise. She had gone to the doctor for a normal checkup late in her pregnancy, expecting only a routine visit. While learning the results from her tests, she could never have prepared herself for the doctor's sobering news. "You have AIDS," he informed her, searching her face for clues. It was in that moment she knew her husband had been leading a double life, for he was the only one to whom she had ever given her heart. His homosexual lifestyle in hidden places had now come into the light. Her life and the life of her baby were placed in jeopardy by an impostor.

More common is the impostor who covers his habits and desires in marriage. Many have come to us over the years who have had sexual cravings and drives they hope will be cured by marriage. Habits practiced in secret breed the artificial life of an impostor. Men who marry to satisfy their growing lust soon look for additional outlets because their lust cannot be satisfied. They reach for x-rated movies, magazines and internet addresses to satisfy their cravings extending beyond the marital status of "happily married."

Some perversions grow with demands from their spouse, compromising safe love and intimacy. The skeptic world watches as men and women are exposed for claiming to be one thing when, in reality, they are something opposite. Impostors who slip back and forth like a Jekyll and Hyde lose their influence on the world around them, leaving it untouched and unmoved by their distorted life-message. Their hearts eventually give them away. The heart of the impostor damages the sincere and the innocent.[2]

Where does it all begin?

Chapter Seven
No Secrets - No Lies

In our home we try to have a "no secrets policy"—unless it has to do with Christmas gifts, birthdays or special surprises.

We believe training children to be lovers of truth is imperative. In addition, valuing a clear conscience and the safety of each family member is of the utmost importance in our home. Therefore, secrets that damage or secrets that hold a life in captivity are to be avoided. Parents, using wisdom and discretion, should serve as a refuge, fielding secrets that could be detrimental and guiding children toward needed resolution. Parents can help children deal honestly with information or experiences that could potentially harm them. Do your children feel safe to come to you with a secret they are carrying in their heart?

One afternoon, a businessman sat busily working on the ever-growing piles of paperwork around his desk. Hearing a knock on his office door and without looking up, he called out, "Come in." Standing in front of his desk was a young man whom he knew well. The businessman warmly greeted him and asked, "What brings you to my office today?" Calling the businessman by his formal name, the young man nervously answered, "I am here to talk about your daughter." The father knew exactly which daughter he was referring to and invited him to have a seat.

The father put away his work and turned his attention to the more important business at hand—his daughter. The young man who had

Engaging the Heart

made this unexpected visit to the office had been a welcome guest in the father's home for many years. In fact, both families had been longtime friends, as well.

"Sir, I am here to discuss my feelings for your daughter." It did not come as a full surprise to the father for he had seen signs of the young man's growing overtures. It was obvious he was fond of her. Though the two of them did many activities together, it was always in the company of others. Her siblings were some of those who often went with them to special events. However, it was now apparent the young visitor wanted more.

The young man indicated he had heard how much the young daughter wanted her father involved when it came to important matters of the heart, and that is why he had come to talk. At the onset, it looked noble and caring. After a time of conversation and the revealing of this young suitor's intentions, the father began to speak. "I have appreciated your friendship with my daughter. She has enjoyed your company and respects your family. However, I know my daughter's heart." Listening closely, the young man never changed expressions and looked intently at the man as he continued to talk.

"I have talked to my daughter about her feelings and goals and she has indicated to me she is not ready for marriage." Pausing for a brief moment, the father continued speaking to the young man. "She enjoys your company, but only as a friend. If you were to reveal how you feel about her, it would drive her away. She is not interested in marriage at this time. There are so many things she yet wants to do with her life." Continuing, the father warned, "There are certain levels of intimacy I do not want you to explore with her. She is not ready." After some small talk and closure of their time together, the

No Secrets - No Lies

meeting ended as abruptly as it had begun.

Days passed and the daughter's heart was protected as her friendship continued with this young man. Her heart was carefree. His heart, however, was out of rhythm as his feelings intensified.

One night, the young man called the young lady's sister and asked if he could meet her for dinner. The sister, unaware of his intentions, agreed, thinking it was just to meet as friends. He began to ask many questions about her sister's feelings about him. She had unwittingly walked into a trap.

"I have feelings for your sister and I think she should know." Surprised by his forwardness, the sister listened as the young man talked. He never mentioned he had days previously met with her father to discuss this matter and had been given specific instructions. Innocent information given unknowingly by the sister helped further his plan. Clueless to his intentions, the sister had unintentionally given the young man a key to the back door, diverting the father who stood at the front gate of his daughter's heart and wishes.

"Where is your sister tonight?" he inquired. Moving quickly with his new information, he called the young lady, saying, "I must talk with you tonight!" Arrangements were made to meet at a coffee shop at a late hour, without his ever considering her previous commitments.

The night had become late when the young man arrived at the appointed meeting place. There she met her friend who made his request seem urgent.

After ordering two cups of Latte, they headed to the outside patio where tables were set up and others were enjoying the night air. He walked out the door first and she walked many feet behind him, opening the door for herself that had already closed after him.

Sitting across from her, he said, "Don't tell your parents about tonight." He was oblivious to the immediate shutting down of the young lady's heart and to the red flags draped everywhere. She became increasingly uneasy as he blurted out, "I have had feelings for you for a long time. I love you."

Shocked at his outburst, she was quiet while he sat back in his chair with his arms folded. He seemed relieved he had revealed the secret he had been keeping from her. She said nothing. Awkwardly, they sat in silence until he finally asked, "What are you thinking?" "I want to go home," she responded.

Walking her to the car and saying goodbye, he watched as she left for home.

After a sleepless night with pacing and tears, she awakened her father before the dawn. Telling him everything, she expressed her anger and feelings of violation that she had not been protected. "My friendship with him is over!" she raged. Upset, the father told her of the young man's visit to his office. "He has dishonored us both and gone against my wishes." The arranged meeting now seemed calculated and deceptive with the classic opener, "Don't tell your parents." The only heart concern of the young man that night was his own.

Relationships are built on trust. When trust is violated, it must by necessity be regained. Secrets violate trust and often have consequences greater than just the present moment.

Secrets are takers and never givers. Secrets often take away the joy of true friendship and fellowship and can adversely affect one's health. Children who are told to keep secrets may be trapped in dangerous circumstances. I know children who were asked to keep friends' secrets about boyfriends, violence in the home, sexual violations and thoughts of suicide. These are not meant for a child to carry. When a child has been victimized, he is typically threatened that, if he tells anyone, he or the ones he loves will be harmed. Secrets hold hearts and lives captive.

A pastor's wife received a phone call one afternoon that left her shocked and speechless. The mother of a teenage daughter identified herself and went on to say she and her daughter were in the doctor's office in need of help. The mother stated, "I have just been given the news my sixteen-year-old daughter is eight months pregnant." The young teen had hidden her pregnant state by wearing larger clothes, sloppy sweatshirts, and binding her stomach. The dazed mother went on to say, "I have also learned who the father is—it is my husband!" How long had the secrets gone on under one roof?

The travesty and horror of hidden secrets of children being fondled and sexually abused are often not only about abducted children, but include households of dysfunction where innocent children carry a secret too large for their hearts to process and where protection is absent. Does anyone care to ask if their children need to talk about a secret they were carrying?

Children should never be asked to keep a secret from their parents. This could mean a child's friend who speaks candidly about thoughts of suicide or one who might be in a compromising relationship he or she doesn't want parents to know about. Tragically, it could involve an adult abusing a child in some manner and demands being made upon the child not to tell. Parental commitment and the promise to protect a child from evil people must be stronger than the fear generated by an abuser. This allows victimized children the safe

Engaging the Heart

place to tell all and walk free of any intimidating darkness. These scenarios, and many others you may know, re-focus us on building households of truth—living transparently and honestly.

After all, our premise is modeling a God who is Truth and who cannot lie. Jesus said, "I am the Way, the Truth and the Life."[1]

A couple was concerned about their daughter's deceptive and boy-crazy ways. When she ran away from home to be with a young man, they were filled with heartache and tears. They could not understand why the daughter would have turned her heart from them. In time, the root of the problem became apparent.

The parents told a secret they had hidden their whole marriage. When they were dating, their parents did not approve of their relationship. In order to manipulate the disapproving parents, they planned on getting pregnant so the parents would be forced to let them get married. They had kept their daughter's real birth date from her all her life. Did their secret now give allowance to their daughter's deceptive ways?

How different the story might have been had they won their daughter's heart by sharing their concerns because of their own mistake and cover-up. Their disapproving reactions to their daughter's choices had merit. They did not want to see her make the same mistakes they had made. The reason for their concern, however, was kept a secret.

There are so many instances of men who have the appearance of being respected husbands and fathers, even being leaders in their churches, yet are leading double lives. Women, too, are caught up in similar scenarios. Their deceit and lies bring sorrow and shame to their whole family when the truth is finally discovered.

No Secrets - No Lies

Post-abortion clients have begun to disclose the horror and suppressed guilt they have carried for many years. Murderers have turned themselves in after years of hiding because the secret was too much to carry. Many have revealed secrets on their death bed, fearing they would journey into eternity with a clogged heart.

Some secrets even shock the world and fill the television and radio talk shows with endless conversation and analysis. People in positions of respect, such as politicians, pastors and priests who have been outspoken on ethics and virtue, generate criticism and fester cynicism when they have been caught living a double life. Traveling business men, professors and school teachers who live one way at home but another when away, brazenly think their conduct will remain undetected. Their inflated egos fool them to believe they can live as double agents, hiding their true identity and secret practices. Do they really think that no one would ever discover their secret? Their practice of living a lie has seared their conscience.

Is it truly a heart of repentance when you are caught in a lie and then forced to admit the truth?

Recent headlines further exposed a famous politician when he was caught lying about his lies. The world mocked his strong stance and platform on family values when they learned of his ongoing adulterous affair. How many have been victimized by all the secrets and lies.

When a child walks in anything but truth, he or she learns to live with a violated conscience. A child who keeps secrets and avoids the clearing of his or her conscience may practice compromising behaviors that might be easily carried into the adult years.

A coach kept files of pornography accessible only to himself

Engaging the Heart

for his own gratification; however, his son privately discovered his father's secret. The fear of his father's reaction, if he confronted him about the damaging material and the heartache it would bring his mother if she knew, kept the young man confused. The constant tension between truth and deception trained him to assume that's how life is—keeping secrets keeps the home safe. Or does it?

Unfortunately, the young man, in time, introduced his teammates to the same vile pictures during a sleep-over one night as he assumed, "This is just what men do." Consequently, an entire team was affected—and a string of households—because of one father's secret. Each member of the ball team now wrestles with the same tension as they individually weigh the consequences of revealing their coach's secret. The ever-increasing layers of secrets and lies erode foundations of both immediate and extended relationships. Is there any wonder the coach became frustrated with a team that seemed to have lost its focus. Mysteriously, he could no longer effectively rally his team, sensing he had lost their cooperation and respect, but never knowing why.

Many homes have been unraveled by the addiction to internet pornography. Countless couples reach out for help to restore the love and intimacy they once had. Many of these had outward appearances of being upstanding moral people in their communities and churches. When the problem was finally confessed through brokenness and tears, their answer came when all the secrets were placed on the table to be sorted out. Ongoing accountability to each other with a "no secrets policy" becomes an effective lifeline out of the sinkhole they have entered.

The Apostle Paul asked, "What fellowship can light have with darkness?"[2] The wrong kind of secrets brings darkness to any home

No Secrets - No Lies

and results in broken relationships and trust, fueling guilt. Secrets isolate and walls are built overnight that oftentimes cannot be penetrated.

Secrets close hearts and can ultimately repel intimacy in marriage, teaching us to live calloused and bound, fearing what truth might bring. Truth is essential for open and healthy hearts. No wonder many long for intimacy in marriage and wonder why it is not accessible.

Secrets lead to lies and lies never find comfort in truth. Tony says, "Many people tell 100% of 50% of the truth." "Keeping a light on" is more than a cute hotel commercial. It is passage to healing and peace and serves as the best accountability policy for an open heart.

Mark 4:22 states: "For there is nothing hidden which will not be revealed, nor has anything been kept secret but that it should come to light."

Your secrets are affecting someone. When do the secrets begin? Where do the lies take over?

Chapter Eight
Crowded Altar

Traveling one June to attend a wedding, a scene of rare beauty unfolded before us. In the majestic mountain range of northeastern Pennsylvania, the hovering clouds softly settled upon part of the mountainside. Casting a shadow over a portion of the mountains, they created contrasting views. Rays of sunshine broke through the clouds at various portals, highlighting the beautiful foliage. The variety of maple and pines, intermingled with oaks and walnut trees, created variegated shades of green. In the shadow of the covering they appeared to be nearly black with intermittent bursts of forest green highlighted by partial sun rays shining through the cover of clouds. The clouds subtly moving across the mountains would inspire any artist to reach for his brush and pallet to capture such picturesque beauty.

I noticed just beyond the clouds was full sunshine on that same mountain range, awaiting its turn to be covered. As I watched from a distance, the top of the mountains seemed to showcase the carpeted terrain of rich green shades of color textured by the differing heights of trees, inviting the admirer to climb its peaks for a breathtaking view.

Awestruck by the landscape, I saw nestled in the valley the peaceful scenes displaying the simple life of years gone by. Amazed it still existed, I looked on. Corn surrounded by new green hay and fields of soybeans resembled a patchwork quilt. Passing by neighboring

CROWDED ALTAR

Amish farms with laundry blowing on the clotheslines and horses in the field, I imagined what life was like before the rush of modern times. Their simplicity displayed a feeling of order and peace. The echoing of birds singing enhanced the perfect setting for our journey. It had become late in the afternoon with the shadows lengthening as we neared our destination—the wedding.

A few miles down the road in a midsize town sat a historic chapel where witnesses were gathering. The day had finally come for a couple who had announced their engagement nine months previously.

Their anticipated marriage seemed like a romance novel with unending love shared. The fading rays of the sun highlighted the flowers along the streets of this quaint town where the wedding was to take place. Family and friends had come to celebrate love. There was an air of excitement among them and a feeling of joy to witness what some called "a marriage made in heaven."

The audience of witnesses lined the steps awaiting a ringside seat for the ceremony of the decade. Everything seemed perfect. Once seated and with the clock nearing five, the mothers of the young couple entered the chapel, walking to their seats of honor.

Entering from the side of the stage was a distinguished looking man with graying temples. Behind him walked a line of handsome gentlemen dressed in tailored shirts and formal vests. Adjusting his posture and position, the groom glanced over the crowd then quickly focused on the double doors at the end of the center aisle. His eyes never moved as he looked for the one who would take his name and pledge her love for a lifetime.

His parents looked on as they remembered their son's youthful

Engaging the Heart

days of school honors, letter jackets, sports trophies and years away at college, finding his own way. Tears welled in both of their eyes as they prepared to expand their hearts to embrace his choice for a wife.

Across the aisle sat the bride's mother, along with her own elderly mother. Both marveled at how fast the years had gone. Numb from all the days of work preparing for such a gala occasion, the mother of the bride relished the moment to simply sit and rest as she pondered her next part in the program. Her only daughter had been worth all the sacrifices and work the last years had brought. Though there had been seasons of indecision and struggle to prove her independence, she finally seemed at peace. She now would soon belong to the man of her dreams. Her unfinished college days had at last secured her a husband.

Music that had been playing softly now intensified with the sound of violins and brass as the bridesmaids appeared from a back room, standing at the threshold of the sanctuary.

On cue, the four maidens and one little girl walked slowly down the white cloth aisle to take their positions near the altar. Their variety of spring-colored chiffon dresses were complimented by the bouquets of fresh cut flowers they carried with lace ribbon draping from their gloved hands. Smiling with innocence, the little flower girl placed her petals along the aisle, covering it like a princess, as her long golden curls swayed with each step. With a sparkle in her eyes, she knew her assignment was to pave the path for the center of attention—the queen of the ball.

Soon the orchestrated music announced with a trumpet sound, "Stand, for the bride is ready to enter." With a sudden hush and in unison, the audience stood to their feet, gazing with awe at the

CROWDED ALTAR

young girl who had become a lovely woman overnight.

The bride's pleasant smile and relaxed stride contrasted with her father's stoic face. His pride of having his daughter at his side was clearly seen. Never would there be a more important processional for them than this one. Together they ushered in the winds of change.

"Who gives this woman to marry this man?" came the riveting question of the ages. "Her mother and I," was the answer heard, spoken with resolute firmness. Kissing his daughter and lingering to look deep into her eyes, the bride's father slipped her hand into the hand of her soon-to-be husband. Her eyes now danced with delight as she turned to gaze deeply into the eyes of the one who had captured her heart. Adjusting the long train of her designer lace gown from the city boutique, she moved closer to the side of her groom as they both now focused on the pastor.

Addressing the crowd of witnesses, the pastor unveiled his text as he proposed the question. "Will you enter into a covenant or contract today?"

Without anyone noticing, shadows of people came from obscure places, finding their rightful positions at the altar. No music played as they came one by one. Several entered by the side aisles. One walked from the back entrance of the stage but none came down the center aisle on the white runner signifying purity. Puzzled, I watched as they played reversed roles to those of the wedding attendants. The women stood on the side of the groom while the men took their places not far from the bride. Each remained in the shadows of the spotlight, yet their presence was strangely felt. They dressed in casual attire, unfitting for the event. Their shadows diminished the brightness of the moment but no one seemed to notice.

Engaging the Heart

Oblivious of the shadows, the pastor read his scripted message and quickly advanced to the exchanging of the vows. A strange feeling of stuffiness came over him as if there were a crowd of people at the altar. He nonchalantly adjusted his collar while the young couple spoke of their love and commitment to each other. Pausing, they each took their turn speaking personalized, handwritten vows that had been masterfully inspired.

"Do you have a ring to signify your never ending love?" the pastor asked. Their favorite love song was played while they exchanged rings, never taking their eyes off one another as they anticipated the finale.

Smiling, the pastor joyfully announced, "You may now kiss your bride." As the audience witnessed their embrace, so did the shadows of the uninvited witnesses. The vows made had been sealed with a passionate kiss and the great exchange was made. Once independently single, now two hearts were blended into one and joined in marriage.

Turning to the watching crowd, the couple prepared to swiftly walk between their families, announcing to them and the world a day of new beginnings. Unaware of the shadows of people that had been in their paths, the exhilarated groom offered his arm to his new bride.

Nothing would ever be the same.

Shadows of the past from unresolved relationships make their presence known in time. A man who has given his heart to his first love is tempted to savor the memory simply because it was his first. A woman who remembers her first kiss can bring back fresh emotions felt from the love experiment. The heart never forgets.

CROWDED ALTAR

A young man once was rejected by the girl of his dreams. Reacting to her rejection, he quickly moved into another relationship to cover his broken heart and disappointment. Unfortunately, the young, unsuspecting girl had no idea she was not his first choice. The world refers to such a relationship as if they were at a basketball game yelling, "Rebound! Rebound!" His heart missed his targeted goal but never came to rest before he tried again to score.

Issues of the heart must be resolved. Previous relationships may hover over the present when emotional heart strings have never been cut. Comparisons, regrets, disappointments and imaginations can steal intimacy from a marriage without even knowing why.

I have heard women say to me, "I cannot get beyond the invisible wall of my husband." Their cry is for intimacy. This is not only on the man's side because a woman can also shut down emotionally when she is overwhelmed or wishing for how the past might have turned out with another she once loved.

Some struggle with random thoughts of another person whom they once cared for and without conscious thought may think of them during a day and wonder how things might have been. Some look to a past relationship for approval, while others look to hurt the one they first gave their heart to because of the pain they once suffered. Shadows of the past that have not been severed remain chained to the present.

Often the children and I would discuss relationships and the potential traps that can be set without noticing them at first glance. One evening while Lindey and I were working in the kitchen, she astounded me with her fifteen-year-old wisdom. As we talked about purity and guarding the heart, she said, "Mom, I am not only interested in keeping myself physically pure, but I also don't want to have any emotional baggage."

Her wise declaration was the basis of a statement I challenged my children with over the years. I challenged them to live life with no regrets. "My desire for you and your siblings is to be able to tell your future children every part of the journey you have walked. Your own love story with your future mate will model for them a more excellent way." Living a life with no regrets helps eliminate the shadows that come uninvited into our lives.

Some husbands have defrauded their wives by crossing over lines of intimacy before marriage. The same can be said of wives toward husbands. More devastating are relationships that have engaged in sexual passion, never planning to marry the one they have physically defrauded. The Bible confirms that "sin is pleasurable for a season"[1] but often disregarded are its effects long-term.

Unconstrained dating and casual sex rob from days yet to come. A couple sat in front of us who were planning to marry in six months. There was always an undercurrent of turmoil and anger that surfaced at the worst of times. We talked with them about character qualities and the differences between men and women. Laughingly, we all tried to imagine the exact distances from Venus and Mars as we referred to a popular book at the time which described how different men and women can be in their mannerisms and thought patterns.

After watching the couple interact with each other, I asked, "What secrets crowd out your future together?" They both began to talk saying they had always shared everything with the other and there were no secrets in their past. All of their lives were an open book for the other to read. Both lives had tasted of moral failures and lost loves. They had not protected their hearts before coming to Christ and had experienced many promiscuous relationships. They had a good sense of being forgiven by the Savior and their new lives in Christ were solid, yet something hung on that wedged itself between their hearts.

While observing and closely listening, I asked, "Have you ever forgiven each other for not protecting and saving your hearts for each other?" Deafening silence filled the room. I went on to say, "You trespassed into another's life with no thought of what was being stolen. It was your own treasures belonging only to each other. You failed to save your heart wholly for this time and now you are groping to find all the pieces from the past to make a whole heart." Their actions had defrauded the other.

Tony and I watched as they faced each other asking forgiveness as they cut off the past. Both began to weep as they were led in forgiving each other and themselves. The shadows of yesterday were dispelled and a heart pure before God and each other paved the way for a marriage with blended hearts. Months later, no shadows crowded their altar as everyone experienced the presence of the Lord of rings who came to celebrate their vows of marriage. Without hesitation, they gave their whole hearts to each other. Only God could heal the past with no scars.

While attending a family conference, a woman spotted a former boyfriend. Once good friends, the nervous awkwardness of being together now with both of their spouses and respective children made the woman long to be somewhere else. Seemingly unaffected by the crossing of old paths, the man was cordial as if meeting a stranger for the first time.

As the woman sat trying to concentrate on the seminar, she was flooded with thoughts of regrets that her heart had been given to him so many years previously. Though she felt violated because her

Engaging the Heart

heart had not been protected as a young woman, she soon began to focus on her own shortcomings and responsibilities for keeping her own heart. A flood of sorrows washed over her as she wished she had not given her heart unwisely to another during those years. She saw the lost days of building relationships with her siblings and missed opportunities delighting in the short years with her parents. With hundreds attending the conference, only one other person in the crowd was tied to her heart and memories. Unsettled, she prayed, "God, give me a moment to cut my heartstrings from this man."

Feeling guilty and distracted from her devoted husband who sat with her and with her children at her side, she agonized over regretting giving her young heart away. God answered her prayer at the afternoon break. Standing alone was the old boyfriend. Without anyone thinking it strange, she went to stand and talk with him. Surprising him with her topic of choice, she called him by name and asked, "Would you please forgive me for giving you my heart? It never belonged to you." Softly, he answered, "Yes." With nothing more being said, she walked away. The kind, yet defining, crossroad had brought an end to the shadow of times gone by. The only thing missing was a reciprocal request, "Would you also please forgive me for taking your heart and not valuing and protecting it?"

The religious mind that wants to adhere to a list of morals falls short of the one who seeks to understand the treasure within the heart. Keeping your heart and mind only enhance the authentic love relationship God will bring to the one who is willing to trust and wait.

God is a God of romance. From the beginning of the Bible He showed us His heart by creating a woman for Adam beyond his imagination. Even in Adam's loneliness, God gave him a woman with whom to walk side by side and heart to heart. Never did God feel crowded out of the equation, for she added to the original plan of having fellowship with the Creator of the Universe. They walked together—until their hearts turned, leaving a dark shadow of regret for a lifetime.

A couple decided to cover the secret of their daughter's real birth date because they feared her ever knowing about her illegitimate birth. Now leaders in the church, with a strong stance on dating and morality, they made plain their hate for impurity. They had become harsh and unbending when it came to their daughter's social life. Their love for her wellbeing and the fear she might make the same mistake in her life caused them to protect the shadow over her life instead of protecting her with truth. It was difficult for them to understand why their daughter was never close to them nor talked openly with them. They existed under the same roof but never connected on a heart level. She grew weary of their judgments. Their fear spoke louder than their words of love while their daughter continued to live in the shadows. Abandoned, with her thoughts and emotions, she was left to navigate on her own. Barely surviving, she turned to friends with whom she shared her heart and deep secrets.

If only they had been honest with their daughter at an appropriate age. If only they had told her of their past moral failures and how God redeemed their lives and marriage by the work of a loving Savior who forgave. Would the outcome have been different? The daughter could have understood their concerns, paving the way for honest communication, exemplified by her parents. They would have been approachable as they made themselves available to her. Talking and praying together would have replaced walls of judgment and fear. The parents' rules bred rebellion in her because she had

Engaging the Heart

no understanding. The very thing they feared was exactly what happened. Modeling the shadow surrounding her parents past—she got pregnant before marriage. Unable to deal with the fear of her parents' reaction, she chose to abort her baby. Her secret remained in the shadows too.

Truth expels shadows. A life-message touches another life and authenticity validates the work of Calvary and His blood that cleanses us from all unrighteousness.

Sitting in an audience one fall, I listened as two women shared openly about their secret abortions. Their choices and the subsequent post-abortive devastation experience riveted the attentive audience. Both stories had the same common threads as they spoke of the silent years of holding on to something that had stolen their peace and joy. One woman talked about the years of feeling alone, contemplating thoughts of suicide, and sharing about frequent night terrors. Her emotions were like a never ending rollercoaster. The dips and the peaks were only filled with endless tears.

Years later, she married and had a family of her own. In what should have been a joyful time, instead, it was overshadowed by depression that could not be removed. She emotionally walled herself off from her two precious children with no ability to give them her full heart. Her husband had managed to live with her during the same cycles of abandonment of emotions, never knowing the why of it all.

In front of an audience, she bravely shared her story for the first time. She explained her pain saying, "How could I love the children I now have when I took the lives of the children before them?" With great composure and a peace she had never known, she said, "I will hold my secret no longer, knowing my life can help other women who are walking through the same pain." Her shadow of regrets had now broken through with light brighter than her past failures. She had come to know the Lord's forgiveness and now had forgiven herself. Her life message was free to reach another life.

Shadows of secrets, lies, moral failures and regrets are obliterated by the light of the cross of Jesus Christ. His forgiveness is measured as far as the "east is from the west."[2] His forgiveness is complete, covering our past, present and future with the ability to "cleanse us from all unrighteousness."[3] Proverbs 4:18 speaks of the new and growing light when it states, "The path of the righteous is like the light of dawn that shines brighter to the full day."[4] When Jesus hung on the cross to die for our sins His work extended horizontally and vertically. He was the Son of God who reconciled us back to the Father. We were enemies of God, but now we are friends. The life sacrificed by Jesus also reconciled us to each other as He hung between men. His work was complete and His heart demonstrated to mankind that "no height, no depth, nor any other created thing shall ever separate us from the love of God."[5]

It will not be in effortless living that shadows are removed. The Bible says that we must "confess our sins, knowing He is faithful and just to forgive us."[6] If any one calls on the Lord Jesus Christ, confessing Him as Lord and believing God raised Him from the dead, he shall be saved.[7] No greater joy could be offered than to have the shadows of our lives removed by the Light of the world—Jesus Christ.

Perhaps, as you have read this chapter, shadows are becoming exposed. May I encourage you at this moment to ask for His help to do the right thing? For some it will be a phone call asking forgiveness and for others a possible visit to the one you have defrauded. Others may realize the complications of going back to events of the past;

Engaging the Heart

the solution to your past is to talk alone with God. May I encourage you to ask the Lord for His wisdom and grace to walk out of the shadows of past failures and be free from the chains that keep you bound from running the race of life in front of you? Only Jesus can liberate you from your captivity.

I love one of the titles of the Savior. He is the Great Redeemer who will redeem your past mistakes and failures. He will redeem the time and the relationships. He is the One who will make your path bright with hope as He has promised never to leave or forsake you.[8]

Pray with me, "Lord Jesus, I give you my past as I come to the cross of Jesus Christ. Cleanse me of all the shadows of my past." Name aloud the secret keeping you bound and has bound others.

"Lord, I ask your forgiveness, knowing you are faithful to forgive me. I confess you to be the Lord of my life. Give me your wisdom and courage to forgive myself. Use my life-message to speak of your work at Calvary. Instruct me in your ways and lead me in paths of righteousness, for your name sake. I lay my past at your feet and, in exchange, walk clothed in your forgiveness. Thank you…thank you."

Shadows are frail, not permanent, once the cause of the shadow has departed. However, there is one shadow you will want to live under, and that is the shadow of the Almighty. Psalm 91 declares, "I will live under the shadow of the Almighty God who is my refuge and strength."[9] Live your life in His shadow of protection and blessings as you learn to live with an authentic heart, open to His goodness and love—forgiven.

Chapter Nine
Heart Strings

Raising four beautiful daughters before having our first son has been a delightful challenge. The girls' unique personalities, different interests and varying levels of hormonal cycles once made Tony feel outnumbered until Connor came along. When you have had only daughters, you don't fully appreciate how different both genders can be. I love the differences. Heart issues are still the same though.

I have encouraged our children to be gracious to young boys and girls because they are someone's son or daughter. I would want the same for my own. Being gracious is an art just like guarding your heart. Both can skillfully be done without being rude, but wisdom with eyes of discernment is to be chosen above all else. It is not just in the dating years guarding your heart is needed. Your heart must be protected when choosing friends. Proverbs states, "He who walks with wise men will be wise, but the companion of fools will be destroyed."[1]

The danger of dating friends is it can ruin a good friendship. I have encouraged the children to honor friends. True friends are like gold and grow more valuable with every day. Some will be friends for only a season while others for a lifetime. Other friends are simply acquaintances and some of them need to be avoided. The levels of friendships are important to know so you can make a wise decision about the time you will invest in them. When dating is in the picture, the friendship can take on a new level of awkwardness,

Engaging the Heart

often pushing the lines of intimacy to the edge long before it is time to fully give your heart to another.

Friends can influence you to reach for new heights or tear down good morals. I have watched over the years while my children have been better friends at times than their close friends were toward them. With any relationship, you see takers and givers. The scriptures set the bar high when it says, "A friend loves at all times."[2]

One time, one of my girls asked, "What should we do if someone seems to like me?" My advice came readily. "Smile and be gracious in your greeting to them—but keep the line moving."

One day as we were sitting together, I had a heart-shaped paper in my hand. I told them about heart issues, especially concerning dating. I asked them, "Girls, if you had a young man you liked and gave him a piece of your heart, what would happen?" They thought as I tore a small piece out of the heart I was holding and let it fall to the floor. While they still watched, I continued. "What if I grew bored with that person and decided to drop them for another love?" Once more, I tore off another piece of the heart and threw the small section on the floor. After several scenarios of giving their heart to a variety of young loves, with more pieces being scattered on the floor, I then asked, "Ladies, what would you have left to give your husband at your wedding?"

They were intrigued by the torn heart with so many missing pieces and holes. I asked again, "Will you have a whole heart to give to your husband one day?" Then I made the same point about our hearts loving the Savior. When we pray for Jesus to come into our heart or sing that He is the Lord of our heart, exactly how much is preserved for His love?

Dating issues have always seemed shallow and dishonest to me. Usually, two people on a date are well groomed, smell their best, look nice, have good manners and put their best foot forward in order to impress each other. It is more revealing to be with a group of people or with two or more families to see true interaction, character, manners and social skills. If a young man is in the presence of his mother, it is revealing to watch how he treats her. The rule of thumb is he will treat his wife like he now treats his mother. The same is true about a young lady and her father.

Siblings can provide a good test of character. One afternoon, Connor and Lydia were in the midst of an escalating argument. Annoyed they could not play peaceably, I called them into the hallway. "Connor and Lydia, I want you to face each other and look closely into each other's eyes." Their faces were taut and angry looking, as I first addressed Connor. "Is this how you will treat your wife one day?" Connor, who has a big tender heart toward family, looked into his sister's eyes as his face softened and sheepishly answered, "No." I continued asking, "Is this how you will treat your daughter one day?" Now, with big tears about to fall, he sincerely said, "No." Explaining, I said, "You both are in training in our home for how to succeed in your own home one day. Lydia was asked similar questions as I encouraged them to protect their hearts toward each other for it would affect their lifelong relationships. Though their ages were young, eight and six, it was timely and important for them to understand what they practice today is preparation for their tomorrows.

It is insightful to see how patient or kind a brother is with his sister and vice versa. In other group settings, observing the behavior of one you might be drawn to is eye opening as he or she demonstrates

Engaging the Heart

leadership qualities and ability to converse. Watching to see if doors are opened for others and if genuine concern is shown is helpful when judging character. The quality of character modeled over time is essential when looking at the real fruit of one's life.

Tony and I were staying with a pastor and his family in St. Marys, Georgia, where we had been ministering. As we sat at the dining room table one Sunday afternoon, a car drove up in front of the house. It was visible to all of us through the large window overlooking the sidewalk and adjoining driveway. Tony and I watched as the young man got out of the car and walked around to open the door for the young lady who was with him.

Offering her his arm, they walked together to the door of the house. We commented, "Wow! How long have they been dating? He is so protective of her." Chuckling, the pastor said, "Oh! That's not his date. That's his sister." We were quite impressed to think he valued his sibling that much. The first hearts to be won are in the family. Our homes are the training ground for our children.

I believe the goal of parents is to win the hearts of their children. The next important issue is to guard them. As we raised our children, we taught them about guarding their hearts. However, I had no idea it would be challenged in our son's elementary years.

During Connor's fifth grade school year we were amused each night at the dinner hour over some story of boy-crazy girls and flirting boys. I never was too subtle when pointing out how ridiculous that seemed, especially at the young age of ten. Nonetheless, he kept us laughing as we saw little children training themselves for the dating years. Always, it was about someone going "steady" and "liking each other." When we asked Connor to tell us what happens when you go "steady" in fifth grade, he said, "Oh, you just stand by each other at recess." Laughing, we would count all the new heart throbs and the other rejected loves of his class. We began to wonder if he had been enrolled in some kind of dating service instead of fifth grade.

During one dinner, though, my laughter stopped when he said he had a note to share with us from a girl at school. Immediately, I responded, "Give me her phone number!" Connor laughed and then read the note aloud. It is one I will never forget. She said, "I write your name in the clouds and the wind blows it away. I write your name in the sand and the ocean washes it away. I write your name in my heart and it never goes away." Now convinced I definitely should take action, I emphatically said, "I am going to school with you tomorrow to find that young girl!" Laughing together, Connor ripped up the note.

Our culture instills the need and desire to date. Haven't you heard, "How will you ever know who is out there if you don't date?" Simple. Stay focused on your preparation for life and your love will be along your path—in time. A mother of a daughter in our Bible School class on "Marriage and Family" advised our student to use her single years to love as many as she could before marriage. She even suggested they be sexually active so her daughter could choose what and who she liked best. Years after heeding her mother's advice, she came to know the Lord Jesus Christ and now was in our class. With tears streaming down her face, she told me one day, "I wish my Mother would have taught me to protect my heart." Even more tragic, her mother was not there to help her daughter sort through the ruins after she left her abandoned, due to her mother's suicide.

To protect your heart is to value it yourself. Steve Green sings a song that states it well: "Guard your heart, guard your heart. Don't

Engaging the Heart

trade it for treasures, don't give it away. Guard your heart, guard your heart. A payment for pleasure is a high price to pay. With a soul that remains sincere and a conscience clear, guard your heart."[3]

Some time ago there was a couple who had been childless for a long time. One day their hearts were overjoyed to have a son born to them whom they named Sam. Interestingly, before he was born they had been given instructions about his upbringing.

From the womb, they had dedicated Sam to the Lord for His purposes and were determined to listen to any instruction the Lord would give them about raising this promised child who brought them endless joy.

As their son grew, it was obvious he would be part of something special, yet they could never have dreamed of his life's assignment. In spite of their early efforts to keep God's specific rules to govern the boy's life and protect him from worldly influences, he began to desire his own way as he grew to be a young adult.

Sam had been traveling when he spotted a certain young lady. Their eyes met and immediately he knew he wanted her for his own. She did not share his faith and they had little in common. She was oblivious to his life purpose or that he had been dedicated to God since a baby. His parents objected to her because of her cultural background and made their disapproval known to Sam. Unmoved, he persisted that his parents arrange for him to not only meet her but also to have her as his wife.

Who knows the full reasons why some parents give in to their children's wishes, especially when it is against their better judgment? But often they do. During the arrangements for the wedding, a big party was thrown for Sam. Since he did not know anyone in the town, his bride's parents picked out thirty companions to join them at the party.

Sam intrigued them all because he liked to tell riddles which they could never understand. After a time, Sam challenged them to a dare. Whoever could figure out his riddle would be the winner of several treasured items; however, if they failed, the treasure pot went to him. His shrewd plan and over confidence provided hope for a nice financial start for his new marriage.

For one week the marriage gala continued as did the challenge of the riddle. Frustrated, the newly appointed friends became like a Mafia gang, threatening the young bride-to-be, saying, "We will burn down your father's house with you in it, if you don't find out the answer to the riddle for us." They feared they would lose the challenge and it would cost them money they did not have.

She knew just how to get her fiancé to give in—she cried and nagged for days until he could take it no more. He told her the riddle's answer, but said, "Even my parents don't know." His secret was not kept by the one to whom he had recently given his heart.

On the last day of the celebration of Sam's wedding, his new buddies came with the answer and demanded he make good his agreement. Angry, he went to another town and killed to get the goods to pay them. Disgusted, Sam left his new fiancée and went back home to live with his parents.

When the father of his fiancée realized Sam was gone, he gave her in marriage to Sam's best man. Weeks later when Sam had finally cooled off, he went back to her only to hear the devastating news.

Over twenty years passed before Samson fell in love again. The woman was Delilah. She, too, was not what she appeared to be and she only used Samson to find out hidden secrets. Her espionage role eventually led to Samson's captivity and, in time, his death.

Crazy as it may sound, it is a true story told in Judges 13-16. Samson was a promised child God ultimately used to deal harshly with the enemies of Israel. However, in the middle of his strength and purpose, two different women came into his life who were never interested in his heart or his well being.

I have heard it said when a couple meets at the altar of marriage, six others show up besides the attendants, flower girl and ring bearer. Those who have been married for any length of time can confirm this fact. Who are the six crowded at the altar to take vows?

On the adorned bride's side is: the bride; the woman the groom thinks he is marrying; and the woman she thinks she is. The same is true of the groom's side: the groom; the man she thinks he is; and the man he thinks he is.

Perhaps this is why God instructed newly married young men in Israel not to be given assignments away from home for one year. This would give couples time to get to know each other. All six personalities and behaviors merging together could be an adjustment.

Dating, as we know it, empowers couples to remain in confusion about their identity. Their marital status looks good on paper, but their hearts are in search of more than a lifetime commitment. Few take the time to know who they are in Christ and feel awkward to be alone, not to mention stand alone on godly convictions.

Over the years, as Tony and I have taught at a Bible school in the Southwest, we have been able to monitor the evolving thoughts about dating and marriage. I am amazed at all the young people who have never been alone because they have had someone's hand or another's arm to hold to as they move from relationship to relationship. The joke of the campus, like most other college campuses, is to find a mate before graduation. In the mad rush, this setting becomes a dating pool for the lonely and unsettled; consequently, the divorce rate is staggering—and tragic.

As the mother of college age children, I challenged my daughters to find their life-purpose and enjoy the single life. They knew beyond a shadow of a doubt I did not mean party till you drop. I meant, within the single years, there is so much that can be done and developed. This season of education, mentoring, and serving is incredibly advantageous. Marriage, by necessity, brings built-in responsibilities and restrictions. So, why is being single so bad?

I remember one day thinking that the scriptures said I could have whatever I wanted, based on John's declaration, "If you ask anything in My name, I will do it."[4] This verse had only one meaning as a young, single, eligible gal. I proceeded to make a list of everything I wanted in my future husband. I kept it in my Bible so God would know it was an important list. Then one day I heard Him softly whisper to my heart, "Are you the wife that would complement such a man?"

Feeling the sting of that moment, I realized I too had some preparation to do. Candidly, there is much on-the-job training when it comes to marriage and relationships. However, His principles never change. They must be the anchor of what our heart desires.

"Guard your heart, guard your heart. Don't trade it for treasures, don't give it away. Guard your heart, guard your heart. A payment for pleasure is a high price to pay. With a soul that remains sincere and a conscience clear, guard your heart."

Chapter Ten
The Exchange

While living in Central Illinois, our pastor complimented my husband one day after church. Admiring our older daughters, he said, "Tony, you have ten-cow women." Without explanation, both men knew his meaning. Our daughters were valuable and their price was "far above rubies." From the age-old practice, ten cows denoted the top price for a suitor to secure an eligible daughter in marriage.

Laughingly, we have always kept this uncommon compliment in our memory bank and said, "If our four daughters are worth ten cows each, then Connor will have forty cows with which to negotiate for his wife one day." This would be perfect, considering inflation. Living in the city, the challenge would be where to house our cows.

I remember hearing about another cow in the classic musical, *Fiddler on the Roof*. The story is about a Jewish poppa, named Tevya, with five unmarried daughters during changing times. His wife Golde increased Tevya's pressures by insisting their eldest daughter, Tzeitel, should be married. Yente, the village matchmaker, arrived to tell Golde that Lazar Wolf, the wealthy butcher, a widower of Tevya's age, wanted to wed Tzeitel. She had reached the age of eligibility and it was customary for the firstborn to be married before the others. Under pressure because of her lack of suitors, Tevya struck a deal one day with the butcher in their small village for his daughter's hand in marriage in exchange for a milk cow. Tevya had

The Exchange

no idea Tzeitel was already in love with her childhood friend, Motel, who was a poor tailor. The poppa struggled between the deal he had made, the heart of his daughter and tradition. By far, ten cows seemed more valuable than that one milk cow—but the value of our daughters is beyond mere wealth.

Years ago when I was single, I traveled to the Middle East with my family and some friends. While visiting Egypt, my dad was approached by an Egyptian man who offered him seven camels for me. While writing this book, I called my dad and asked, "Dad, why didn't you take his offer?" Dad quickly responded, "I'm still kicking myself for turning him down!" Humorous as it seemed on the surface, I wondered if seven camels from Egypt was top price like the ten cows from the Midwest.

In Bible times, Jacob invested fourteen years for the girl of his dreams. His story of being cheated by Rachel's father, Laban, could have driven any man away or caused him to become disinterested. Instead of receiving Rachel, after working for Laban seven years as had been promised, a surprise switch was made and, instead, he received Leah because she was the older daughter. Though he was upset by Laban's trickery, he agreed to work seven more years in order to also have Rachel. He pledged to do whatever he could to win the heart of his choice.[1] Love costs something of value.

One day, Connor and I were sitting at the kitchen table. Being very reflective for a ten year old, he asked, "Mom, can we talk?" Discerning he was deep in thought, I answered, "Sure. What's on your mind?" "Mom, what do you say to the father of a girl you are interested in?" Searching my mind for what girl he could be fond of at school and trying not to smile, I paused to take time to think. Never did I want him to know I was shocked by his question at this young age. I never dreamed he would love anyone or anything but his mom, sisters and baseball until he grew whiskers one day.

Speaking slowly, not wanting to wound his tender heart, I thought of every hard challenge I could relay in hopes of discouraging him from ever thinking about a girl again until he was out of college. "Well, Connor, you would need to call her father and make an appointment to talk with him. Then you would need to tell him your intentions regarding his daughter." I never turned my eyes from his face while he sat looking very serious and staring out the kitchen bay window. I continued, "Then you would need to show him how much money you had saved so he would know you could provide for her if you married her." I managed to think of every kind of hoop for him to jump through in hopes it would quench any romantic tug of his heart growing at such a young age.

We sat quietly and then he asked, "But Mom! How is it going to work with the cows?" I looked at his innocent face as I wanted to cry and laugh at the same time. "Hey, Connor Mac, God will give you the favor and wisdom how to win the heart of your future wife when it's time." Satisfied, he got up from the table and hugged me. "Mom, I'm going out to play ball." That was his choice—for now, at least.

Thinking back to the years when we first moved our family to Dallas, we were amazed they seemed to have gone by like a blur. We had always been in full-time work serving the Lord: pastoring for several years; starting a Christian school; hosting a Christian television show; and traveling with the family, as we combined teaching and musical gifts to bless audiences around the United States. They all had been some of the joys of being a family. Our children were five miracle gifts because the doctors said we would probably never have any children. Helping families and seeing them

The Exchange

succeed was our passion, and His faithfulness to the McWilliams family had been evident.

It had been six years since we moved to Texas from the Midwest. More than just the climates had changed for our family. We had been given new friends and new opportunities, and our life-vision had expanded as we began to work with a Bible school in Dallas. Our culture, housing, trials and focus had changed, but not our principles. They were the anchor fitting for every situation and season.

Our oldest daughters were nearing college age, and our two youngest children were six and four at the time of our move. While in our transition, Anna was the first to become a student at Christ For The Nations Institute, with her two sisters following her. Our home was filled with new activities, friends and students. Some friends were only for that season but many would become lifelong friends. Our front entrance seemed like a revolving door with new faces and needs. Among our visitors were many eligible young male students, conveniently the same age as our daughters. Our family was always together, so we included them and made memories around our table.

Sometimes, there would be courageous young lads who would linger, with an interest in one of our daughters. However, most just fell in love with our family. A watchful eye was always over Anna or Lindey, and soon Holly, as admirers came.

Upon occasion, we knew immediately when a "Wickham" would knock on our door. Self-centeredness and immaturity knocked, too, but never had a "Boaz" come—yet. He was the one in the scriptures of old. In the Bible, one of the most beautiful love stories of all is told in the Book of Ruth. Her faithfulness and loyalty in the midst of her crisis led her, in time, to her beloved husband, Boaz, who was kind, generous, wise and prosperous. Her Boaz had become the dream standard for our girls' spouses.

We quickly learned the making of a "Boaz." It is not necessarily his perfect ways or bank account, but the true treasure is his teachable heart. This attribute alone far exceeds the most polished young man. Such a teachable man entered our lives quietly and became a friend of the entire family.

One day when Tony was at work, he received a call he had expected sometime in his life. "Tony, I was wondering if we could meet for lunch today?" asked the caller. Tony agreed. He knew this next season of his life was unscripted and his heart was proof as it began to beat faster. Tony went back to work, but he found it hard to concentrate. Everything he had believed and taught to others was about to be tried.

Lindey and Holly were close in age and activities, being only twenty months apart. At times, it was like raising twins who had similar interests, yet they were uniquely different in other ways. They had joint friends in many circles and did most things together. We loved the fact they were built-in accountability partners. They both loved to socialize and never met any strangers.

Lindey and Holly were always busy with worship teams and music practices on campus and at church. It was in this setting they met Ryan.

Ryan was a tall, kind, but quiet guitarist who played a key role in the worship band. His family was actively involved in the church, and they were the first family to invite us to their home when we moved to Dallas. It was for a wonderful Thanksgiving dinner.

The only thing I remember about Ryan that day was his quietness

The Exchange

and his ability to make a great cup of coffee. He remained to himself, and we found out why much later. He was annoyed his mother had invited a large family with so many single girls to the Thanksgiving dinner. He was leery of his mother's motives and feared being set up. Nothing could have been further from the truth, for our girls were on guard, too, and they had no interest in anyone.

Over the months, Lindey and Holly got to know Ryan better because they all were on the same youth worship team at church. After the church services were over many would go out together to get a bite to eat at a local restaurant.

Lindey said once, "I never wanted Ryan's phone number in my cell phone because I did not want to be like some of his admirers." She had no desire or attraction to be with Ryan except on the worship team. Their positions soon made it necessary to talk because Lindey was appointed the vocal leader and Ryan the band leader. Both leaders were forced to work together.

Any extra outing was always with Lindey, Holly and Ryan, like a trio. They were the threesome that could not be separated. With shared interests, stimulating conversations and growing leadership qualities, best friends grew to respect each other.

The months turned into years and Ryan's family asked us each year to join their full house of company for Thanksgiving. Ryan was still quiet in some ways but more comfortable with our family who had become his friends, too. His gentle ways, thoughtfulness and quiet leadership were admired as we watched this young man grow to be more confident in who he was in Christ.

After some time, having Ryan around had become the norm. However, the phone call Tony now received from Ryan seemed potentially different than before. The two decided on a nearby fast-food restaurant in the busyness of a mall food court to discuss what was on Ryan's heart. The lunch was anything but fast.

Ryan ordered a value-sized sweet tea, anticipating, perhaps, an elongated lunch with Tony. After prayer together, Ryan said he wanted to discuss Lindey. Tony asked, "Ryan, what are your intentions with my daughter?" From there both men began six months of weekly meetings to discuss life, choices, discipleship and, most important, one's identity in Christ. A teachable "Boaz" had come and his heart was fully open.

A surprise gift for our daughter was being packaged to be exchanged for a special day yet to come.

Tony told Ryan he would not tell Lindey the two of them were meeting together until a time that would be appropriate, and asked him to do the same. Tony wanted to protect Lindey's heart and thoughts and, most of all, protect her close friendship with Ryan. He was concerned, if Lindey knew about the meetings, she may feel awkward or be tempted to prematurely enter into levels of intimacy. The decision proved to be wise. Assessing the magnitude of this series of events, my husband shared with me the discretion we needed to exercise during this time. Together, we prayerfully took on the role of overseeing information to protect our daughter until a time that it was safe and prudent to reveal it.

Over the next months nothing appeared to change with Lindey's heart. Her heart had been guarded for so long, but now she began to feel tinges of desiring to open it to Ryan. Lindey became concerned because she had never felt like this before, and she desired her father to be involved in the process.

The Exchange

Seeing Lindey's quandary, I asked her one afternoon, "Are you falling in love with someone?" Smiling and looking at me she said, "I would have to lose my footing first." Smiling back at her, I knew her heart was still safe—but the season was about to change.

Though we had taught the girls in principle, we now had the privilege of applying it in real life, and we all wondered how it would work exactly. We needed the Lord's help and His daily wisdom. Just because you open your heart to someone does not guarantee a happy outcome.

Over the years, I have seen the best of friends lose their friendship when the relationship turned an abrupt corner and become a potential love. Dating frequently ruins the best of friendships because, when the experiment is over, there is an awkwardness that usually remains. The friendship is never the same.

Three months into Tony and Ryan's routine weekly meetings and lunches, it was nearing Valentines' Day. Ryan e-mailed Tony to ask for his blessing and tell him of his wishes. He desired to take Lindey to a very nice restaurant, alone. He did not want to jeopardize the trust or carefree friendship with Lindey by implying there was more. And yet, more was mounting with each passing week. Tony was appreciative of Ryan's thoughtfulness and of his honoring Tony's desire to protect Lindey's heart. He proved in this one action that Ryan, too, knew how to protect. Tony consented to his request with an e-mail response. It said, "I don't mind that you would plan something around Valentine's Day with Lindey. I believe Lindey would like that. I trust you to make it special enough to create a memory and discreet enough to keep your two hearts 'tame'."

In the meantime, Lindey had become more and more restless. Her feelings were starting to grow for Ryan beyond the friendship they had enjoyed. She struggled with her new feelings and emotions as she longed for her Dad's involvement and blessing. Though they had been talking often about her interests and what Lindey desired in a husband one day, it had not yet been revealed someone was in the waiting.

Exasperated, Lindey came to our bedroom one night and said to me, "How will any interested man know to come to Dad?" Listening to her fear, I answered, "Lindey, how do you know someone has not already come?" She suddenly got very still and replied, "I don't know." Smiling, she came to hug me goodnight. "Lindey, you can trust."

Trust is a major factor when learning to love and giving your heart to someone else. Trusting the Lord must come first. Psalm 139 assures us that He knows us better than we know ourselves. Yet, we don't trust Him to pick out our mate. We often think we have to manipulate the circumstances or search on our own. I have heard it said, "I am the one who is going to have to live with my mate. I should be the one to pick out who I want." Is "picking out the one" really the only issue or are there other vital issues you must consider?

Not all couples are examples of this, however. What about the couples who "have to get married" due to an untimely pregnancy, proving they enjoyed the honeymoon before the wedding was even a thought? Did they choose or were they forced to marry? What about the couples who were lonely and took matters into their own hands, never regarding any thought of their life-assignments or plan of God? What about the couples who married for security and not love? What about the couples who married because of lust and attraction but never learned to be friends? Is there a more excellent

The Exchange

way?

One story does not an expert make, but I do know His ways work. One evening a few days before the Valentines' Day outing, when Lindey was cutting Tony's hair, he announced, "Lindey, I have been talking with Ryan over the past several months about you." He immediately had her undivided attention, as she continued to cut with precision. "Ryan has asked me for permission to take you for a special outing alone. I told him 'yes'—if it is alright with you and you are interested."

Lindey changed right before our eyes. The queen of ice and the master of guarding her heart had been given permission to begin to open her heart. The shut up fragrance of fresh smelling flowers gradually opening their petals was nothing compared to the beautiful fragrance that began to come from our daughter's heart. She became giddy and childlike as she hugged her Dad and said, "Thank you."

Ryan and Lindey, along with both families, began to seek God's will for their futures. Tony set guidelines for their path that he asked them both to honor. Though they were young adults, they willingly embraced Tony's wisdom for they had come to trust him, too. One thing Tony asked of them both was to use discretion and refrain from words of intimacy like, "I love you." They were asked this separately. Those words advanced levels of intimacy that were not appropriate for this particular season. He wisely asked them to save those words. The focus was in getting to know each other. Special times with both sides of the families brought new memories. Wisely, Ryan took each of Lindey's siblings individually to a special outing he had planned so they might get to know one another better. Even I was included in his thoughtfulness. The days of discovery were priceless.

It became comical as everyone began to explore the word "like" instead of "love." Ryan and Lindey would sit on the "like seat" with lots of "like" in the air and listening to "like" songs. My favorite was when our family would tell Ryan goodbye from the front door yelling, "Bye, Ryan. We love you." Lindey would wave and say, "Bye, Ryan, I like you." It was fun as we all worked as a team protecting both of their hearts.

On the night of the Valentines' date, Lindey brought a gift to Ryan that became their favorite. It was a children's book called, *I Like You*.[2] Sitting on the couch in the lobby of the restaurant, Lindey read the book aloud to her dearest friend. I am sure the author of that simple little book had no idea of its new market. The book was perfect and time was given for two hearts to find genuine love.

Tony and Ryan kept meeting together as Lindey and Ryan's hearts were opening to each other. With both families involved and with loving prayerful support, they navigated through unknown waters unharmed and remained the best of friends.

One day six months after Tony and Ryan began their weekly lunches, Tony received another call from Ryan asking if they could meet at Starbucks for coffee. Though Tony does not like coffee, he liked Ryan, and the meeting place seemed perfect as two friends met to talk.

After some casual conversation, Ryan began by saying, "Tony, I don't have any cows to offer you." Tony began to laugh and asked if Ryan knew our family story about the cows. Ryan had never heard about the pastor in Illinois who had originated the story about the "ten cows" years ago. Tony enjoyed sharing it with him, and then regained the seriousness of the moment. Looking Ryan in the eyes, he asked, "Ryan, what do you have to offer?" As the moment seemed

The Exchange

to stand still and they looked face to face, Ryan replied, "I have a life and a lifetime." He continued by saying, "Tony, I would like to take Lindey on a day date with the sole purpose of asking her to be my wife. May I have your blessing?" Tony was not caught by surprise by such a request because he had walked the last six months with a man he now admired and trusted. Smiling, and with a poppa's satisfaction, Tony gave his blessing.

Walking away from the meeting, Tony almost forgot to give one more timely directive. "Hey, Ryan! You are free to now use the words 'I love you.'" Ryan smiled in full agreement. Now he could focus on the long awaited day of the engagement—at Central Park, New York City. The father's blessing had paved the way.

Only God could have orchestrated on His Daytimer® the exact events of the journey to New York City. Never before had Tony and Ryan's father, Raymond, been together in the afternoon. However, the day Ryan and Lindey flew to New York for the day outing and surprise engagement, the two fathers were traveling to Fort Worth on a joint errand.

Raymond first received a text message from his son which said, "I did it. She said, 'Yes!'" Moments later Tony, too, received a text from our daughter saying, "He did it. I said, 'Yes!'"

Both fathers laughed as they rejoiced over the news. Within minutes, Raymond suggested another surprise. "Tony, let's meet our children tonight at the airport when they arrive home." Eagerly, Tony agreed.

What fun it was to travel together to the airport at midnight, with Connor alongside to take pictures of the newly engaged couple.

Ryan's mother, Cindy, and I sat waiting in the terminal calmly talking about weddings while the two fathers kept checking the doors where the anticipated engaged couple would enter. Soon, Raymond saw them coming and we all sprang to our feet to welcome them home. Smiling and with hugs for everyone, the exhausted couple were quick to show us their engagement ring while telling us about their whirlwind day. Connor flashed pictures nonstop to fill several scrap books.

With a wedding yet to be planned, the two families felt the smile of God for the next generation.

Chapter Eleven
The Kiss

One morning in Mrs. Yeakel's kindergarten class, Holly was sitting at her desk, having just come in from recess. Normally, she was one of the last to be seated, but this morning she decided to try something new and go straight to her seat. As she sat there, one of the young boys in her class came by her desk and laid a big kiss right on her lips. Stunned and disgusted, she quickly wiped her lips off. She sat very still for the rest of the class, thinking, "Boys are gross!" What provoked such a random action from a five-year-old?

A twelve-year-old girl spent two weeks at a church camp. The ages were mixed from junior high through high school. One night after chapel service, an older male teen, seventeen years of age, approached her after the meeting when no one was around. Though strangers, he talked with her for a brief moment, indicating he might be interested in her, and then leaned in and kissed her. Leaving after the kiss, she wondered what exactly had just happened. She never asked for any affection nor could she hardly believe what had just taken place. Her innocence was taken with a kiss in the night awakening emotions prematurely.

Two teens stood outside our campus apartment window, unaware anyone was listening to their conversation. The young teen said to the apprehensive girl, "What? You have never been kissed by a boy?" She replied, "No." Standing on the inside of the large window, not meaning to eavesdrop, was Holly, trying not to laugh. The boy instructed, "Just close your eyes. It won't hurt." Holly reached for the blinds to open them suddenly only to add to the drama of the moment and expose their secret.

When teaching our daughters as they were growing up, I would offer advice to them saying, "Work for a righteous conclusion in every area of your life." This could apply to unresolved arguments, unforgiveness, injustice or misunderstandings. Passion is the same.

When a male and female begin to arouse passion, where can it go safely? The danger of arousing passion early in your life can leave you wanting more and more. Kissing is one of the most sensual starting places for emotional and, sometimes, moral conflict before marriage. Kissing can lead to other slippery slopes.

Secret kisses in the night and blatant kisses in the daylight all have the potential for awaking a sleeping giant within—passion. Casual kissing and passionate kissing all start the same way. A young girl can connect her heart to every kiss that comes her way, in contrast to a young man who can give a good night kiss and never mean anything by it. To kiss or not to kiss is not as concerning to me as the question, "What passions are stirred and where will they lead?"

For example, if you are the type who kisses on every date, where does that kiss lead? If it arouses emotions lying dormant, how can that end in a "righteous conclusion." Stirred up passion looks for an outlet where it can be satisfied.

What about the young man who can kiss any girl and not have it mean anything more than a weak handshake. The girl, however, may take his unfeeling kiss to mean much more. Often a woman is ready to give her heart long before a man is willing to open his, let alone give it. Where is the "righteous conclusion?" or more clearly,

The Kiss

"What is the right conduct that is sincere and honest?"

Is the passion of the moment excusable with secret words whispered, having little or no meaning the next morning? The modern term "players" is descriptive of many who play with emotions, hearts and promises that end empty. Kissing is one of the most passionate exchanges of all. Females, especially, can entice a young man with her kisses and her immodest clothing, leaving a man aroused with no "righteous conclusion." The man of Proverbs was warned about a promiscuous young woman, saying she was like "taking fire to his bosom."[1] Paraphrased, something is going to burn with passion.

When our first married daughter became engaged, we talked about her childhood wish of having her first kiss be at her wedding. She wanted to give her first kiss at the right time to the one who would have her heart for a lifetime. I cautioned her that some may not honor her wish and try to steal kisses or make fun of her heart's desire.

In helping Lindey keep her wish, I often role played with her. I asked her in her younger years to imagine being proposed to one day by the one she loved. "What will you do when you want to kiss him then?" I asked. We discussed the different emotions and temptations that might skew her heart's intent. I continued by asking, "What about the day your fiancé gives you a beautiful ring? In appreciation, you will possibly want to thank him with a kiss." Once more, she would think through the emotions of those moments and reaffirm her decision to save her first kiss for her husband. The keepsake of that moment was worth treasuring.

One imaginary scenario was of a young man who had spent over a hundred dollars on a date that would be filled with memories and possible romance. I asked, "What if your date thought your kisses would be payment for the obligation you might feel as he spent his hard earned money on you?" Repulsed by the thought of affection as payment for money, she thought it sounded like the profession of a prostitute. It devalued the kiss. I talked about every possible scenario as I walked her through situations where she might feel the pressure to compromise her heart's desire.

I believe the respect I had for our son-in-law, Ryan, came first when he honored our wishes as a family and when he honored Lindey's wish to save their first kiss for their wedding day. He liked the idea, though it had been a new one to him.

Days after their November wedding, I sent the E-mail below to some friends. From my view, the wedding confirmed a lifetime of teaching and heart to heart talks about love and marriage.

Friday, November 10, 2006.

Mazel Tov, Ryan and Lindey!

We have a married daughter!! Where did the years go?

On Friday night, November 10, 2006, our daughter, Lindey, was married to Ryan. We are still smiling over the blessing of the Lord. It was an incredible night as we celebrated the covenant of marriage.

The wedding took place in north Dallas at Lindey and Ryan's home church, Bent Tree Bible Fellowship. It was a ceremony that was "out of the box" and built on the right priorities. Lindey wore a gown she had found in Dallas that was the only one in the nation like it and almost exactly like the one she had sketched since a young girl. The ivory satin

The Kiss

dress was straight fitting with a beige band at the waist and a short sweeping train. She carried a beautiful vintage book of vows instead of flowers and wore no veil. Her adornment was a perfect antique necklace she had found recently while ministering in Austin, and she wore her favorite deep crimson heels. Lindey looked stunning and would have made the front page of any uptown bridal magazine or society page with her fresh look and bold statement that weddings can be all about your own choice and style.

Ryan wore a suit designed with a European fit. Together, the bridal couple complimented each other like models, yet this wedding was far from mere fashion statements. Their focus was the commitment of covenant and personal vows they each had written and a full program of lasting memories.

The members of the wedding party were called "witnesses" and consisted of all of their siblings: three sisters and two brothers. Each male wore a black suit with cream shirts and no ties. Each sister wore black evening attire of her choice. The mother of the bride, yours truly, wore a shimmering copper-colored fitted gown and the mother of the groom wore an elegant knee-length, rust-colored jacket with black blouse and tapered black slacks.

The service started thirty minutes late because the parents of the groom were tied up in major traffic only ten minutes from the church. God used this delay to allow many others to not miss the wedding because of the terribly dense traffic of Dallas this particular Friday night. The people kept coming in large numbers so God knew the audience was not positioned yet for His event. On arrival, everyone mingled like at a church service with no one being ushered in but only greeted and given freedom to take their places with either family.

The decorations were beautiful with many large globe shades with pale blue lights hanging majestically under a canopy of long swags of ivory fabric draped from the sides of the room to the center. All of this, along with the special stage lighting, created an awesome setting. The decorations were another special blessing of the Lord to Ryan and Lindey. While they were in Brazil on their Amazon outreach, the church hosted a mission's conference and decorated the auditorium like described. The church graciously left the decorations up for the wedding. It was another display of God's favor toward Ryan and Lindey for putting Him first by choosing to be part of the mission trip during the last weeks of planning their wedding. The foyer was also beautifully decorated with soft up-lighting under tall branches Ryan's mother designed and arranged, along with a large framed picture of Ryan and Lindey.

After the grandparents walked to their seats, the heart warming DVD of Lindey and Ryan was shown as they told their story of the events leading up to this evening. Sharing back and forth between them, they each told their side. Ryan told how he had approached Lindey's father and met weekly with him for six months before Lindey even knew. They recaptured their first meeting, their first interest much later, their day date to New York City with the surprise engagement, and their being released to finally say, "I love you."

The processional started with Ryan leading the way, carrying his own vow book. Tony and I followed him down the

The Kiss

center aisle while high-energy music played, called "Never Alone" by New Zealand artist, Julia Grace. Ryan's parents then entered with the siblings coming after them. In addition, the three pastors with their wives followed as part of the united front to declare, "Let the marriage begin." During the bridge of the song, Ryan's little niece came down the aisle, placing colored fall leaves as she walked.

As the music began to build on the same song that all had walked in on, Lindey entered the aisle holding her father's hand and walked briskly and confidently down the aisle. The crowd began to applaud as they walked, in anticipation of the destined union. It was a powerful statement long before the first word was uttered.

The siblings stood on stage to the audience's left while the three pastors stood to the back center. All faced the audience. My dad and Ryan's dad were to the front of the stage on the left, Tony stood on the right with Ryan, and Lindey was in the center. After the grandfather and fathers exited the stage, the participating pastors each came forward one at a time to give their message to Ryan and Lindey.

The covenant celebration started with Lindey's grandfather, my dad, greeting the audience and speaking blessings over them and the ceremony. My father then asked my husband, "Who gives this woman to be married to this man?" Tony made a statement about how Ryan had demonstrated great honor and respect for our family. He said it was "without reserve" that Gail and I happily deliver Lindey to Ryan in this covenant setting. Tony joined his daughter's hand into his new son's hand and stepped to the side to continue. Then Ryan's father,

Engaging the Heart

Raymond, spoke a blessing over the couple and Tony followed by speaking the blessing from the scriptures the McWilliams family have become known for giving that begins, "May the Lord bless and keep you..."[2] Tony then instructed the new couple to look over the crowd of friends and family who had come to engage in the night of vows, as a song Lindey wrote and sang was played, based on Romans 8. It beautifully stated "all things work together for good for those who love Him."[3]

Each pastor from the Houston area, dear covenant friends of Lindey and Ryan's, had an assignment to address the couple and audience. Pastor Chuck Colegrove spoke first to explain the importance of the covenant and its lifelong ramifications. Next, Pastor Nathan Keller spoke of the witness and led the congregation in a public declaration to pray and watch over this loved couple. Finally, Pastor Kevin Herrin spoke of three kinds of marriages in relationship to Jesus and his first wedding attendance. The first marriage he spoke about begins with the best wine, but it quickly dissolves. The second marriage begins with good wine but soon it is watered down with a lack of respect and love leaving a bad taste in the mouth throughout the years. The third marriage is one that begins with good wine but the best wine is yet to come. He encouraged everyone, as he charged the marriage couple, to always ask for Jesus to put His hand in their wine—their marriage. Then he led Lindey and Ryan in taking communion, as all were reminded of the ultimate covenant and sacrificial love and commitment shown to mankind.

The song "Great is Thy Faithfulness" was sung by special friends, Scott and Vonda Dyer, who asked the congregation

The Kiss

to join them in singing toward the end of the song. Ryan and Lindey then shared their original handwritten vows, crafted by two people who knew who they were in Christ. Exchanging rings, the two faced each other with everyone witnessing a depth of love and friendship the previous months had afforded them. Suddenly, the challenge of guarding their hearts and saving their first kiss together for the altar paled in comparison to witnessing hearts that were fully given in a love covenant of marriage.

Still to this moment, I find my husband laughing over what took place next. As the music played and the anticipated suspense grew for the moment the couple would share their first kiss, Pastor Kevin Herrin began to slowly build up to the moment with his words of permission for Ryan to now kiss his wife. Unexpectedly, and seemingly from out of nowhere, Lindey pulled out a nicely folded tissue and began to rub off her lipstick. At the same time, Ryan took a breath mint from his pocket and popped it into his mouth as the crowd began to laugh. As the long awaited kiss was now appropriate, the couple had staged their preparations and obvious desires. Tony and I stood to lead in a standing ovation for the covenant that had now been sealed with a kiss. And Connor, age 10, said, "Wow! That was the longest kiss I have ever seen!"

Congratulations! May you be effective in your generation as you serve Him and each other. The best wine is yet to come!

Rejoicing,

McMother of the Bride

One thing Lindey said one day has been imprinted in my heart forever. She said, "Most plan for a fairytale wedding and invest so much in the day. I have determined to plan for a life and enjoy the event." And so we all did!

We have always joyfully anticipated the day our children would marry. Each will have their own story to tell totally different from the others. The principles will remain the same but expressed in different times and places with treasured memories of their own.

No one ever told us how hard it would be to watch one of your own marry. Of course, I am happy for Lindey and Ryan and I have seen the blessing of the Lord over and over. And I eagerly await the new additions yet to come to our family. I must adjust to the fact they are not under our roof any longer or sitting at our table. They now have a table of their own. Soon it will fill with my grandchildren and, for sure, that will be a delight! Whatever the next season, the Lord has been faithful to us and His presence has been seen by all.

We have clearly entered uncharted waters for this McFamily but look forward to the deep treasures that are just beyond. The greatest satisfaction of all is knowing the ways of God work! His blood renews and cleanses and His redeeming love is endless. Marriage is so much more than a license—it is a covenant requiring our lives. Marriage remains a mystery, yet ever so wonderful are the parts we do understand. Having a life partner to now do ten times the damage to the kingdom of darkness and be more effective for God's purposes is reflected in the verses, "One shall put a thousand to flight but two will put ten thousand to flight."[4]

"May He grant you according to your heart's desire and fulfill all your purpose."[5]

Chapter Twelve
Covenant Love

Tony and I have taught "Marriage and Family" at an international Bible school for several years. Our desire is for our students to learn God's principles from which to ask the right questions for success in life. It is not just to give out formulas or simply to show PowerPoint® presentations, giving them mere academic answers.

Tony is the foundational teacher, and I encourage personal application as we look at God's Word. We have created sessions with exercises requiring transparency as the students look into their own lives. Often, we interview our students and regularly try to fill classes with interaction. One morning, there were several students participating on the stage as we worked through an exercise highlighting character flaws and how they might affect the marriage and children yet to come. It was during one of these sessions a profound question was asked by my husband to a female student.

One young lady always masked her answers with streaming tears. Both Tony and I perceived her routine of tears kept her from being real with us as we asked penetrating questions. Tony challenged her to simply talk and resist crying for the time being, so, hopefully, we could help her see something valuable. Showing irritation, she began to show her true self.

Knowing she was engaged and planning to be married that spring, Tony asked, "How long have you been planning your wedding?" She quickly replied, "All of my life."

Engaging the Heart

Pausing for a few seconds, Tony continued questioning, "How long have you been planning for a marriage?" There was no answer.

What ingredients make for a marriage enduring the changing seasons and undercurrents of life? Is marriage only about repeated vows and promised love sealed with a kiss? What deepens heartfelt commitment beyond the marriage license and ceremonial ritual?

Preparing yourself and giving your heart away in marriage are vital. Some argue marriage is only a piece of paper, a license, and an unneeded expense. Others view it as merely a contract with loopholes making for an easy exit. Have you ever considered marriage is a covenant?

Typically, in an American wedding, the audience helps demonstrate a covenant setting. The bride's family is seated on one side of the auditorium and the groom's on the other. After exchanging vows and the pronouncement of marriage, the couple walks through the middle of the family blood lines—the relatives—as husband and wife. This defines a place of blood the bride and groom pass between to begin their marriage covenant.

When the vows are recited and commitment is pledged by penetrating questions, a serious challenge becomes the threshold of covenant love. "Will you take this man or woman for better or for worse; for richer or for poorer; in sickness or in health; till death do you part?" It sounds more serious than, "Will you love me as long as I love you?"

A Vietnam soldier entrapped in the war zone found his life and marriage threatened in fleeting seconds. As part of a Special Forces unit, he attempted to throw a phosphorus grenade toward an enemy target. The grenade exploded in his hand and burned him beyond recognition. He lost his right ear, his nose and some fingers, and his right eye was blinded. Initially assumed to be dead, the valiant soldier was eventually rescued with the doctors giving him no hope.

In time, the soldier was placed in a stateside hospital where he underwent multiple surgeries and constant care for fourteen months. With his face blown off and body parts mutilated and burned, he lay wishing he had not been saved. Death would have been a relief. Later, the soldier's wife walked into the burn ward. She read the hospital chart on his bed confirming it was her husband. In Dave Roever's own words he tells what covenant love looks like. "From the waist up I was charred black. The stench was nauseating. Now my wife entered. She walked straight to my bed and bent over my horrible form." Leaning over to kiss him, she said, "I want you to know I love you. Welcome home, Davey."[1]

His hospital roommate had experienced similar devastation and lay disabled by his injuries and misfortune. Two men had served their country selflessly. Two husbands, however, had different homecomings with their wives.

The man who lost most of his face was met by a wife determined to stand by his side and love unconditionally. The other man's wife came to see him only to take her wedding ring off and lay it on his hospital bed between his charred feet as she walked out. What could have made the difference?

One wife demonstrated unfaltering commitment as she found grace to look beyond the shattered pieces and hold fast to her vow of love. The other wife could only see the inconvenience of life interrupted. One loved unconditionally while the other excused herself from any vow due to the present hardship. One stood in covenant love, while the other broke a marriage contract.

Engaging the Heart

Similarly, a husband lovingly cared for his wife for over two decades as she endured the early onset and the plague of a fading mind taken by Alzheimer's. Even when his wife of forty years could no longer feed or dress herself or perform her daily functions, he stood by her side, loving her, based on his commitment and vow of love. His eyes, filled with compassion and concern, were met with empty stares like a total stranger. She no longer knew her husband nor could she respond to his love. What made the difference between loving her when she could return his love and loving her when she could not?

One of my favorite words is the word "covenant." Several have told me this word is extremely old-fashioned and no one uses it anymore. Perhaps it is time we bring the word back, for it speaks of more than we could possibly imagine.

God was the first to demonstrate the covenant in the scriptures of old. Abram was chosen to be the beneficiary. Upon God's request, Abram was given a specific list of elements that would be needed to establish this covenant. They involved blood.[2]

God walked between the halves of slaughtered animals to display his steadfast promises and covenant love demonstrating the sacrifice of committed love to Abram and his descendants. This relationship was beyond any contract or temporary friendship; instead, it was an enduring love, never wavering. It was not just a mere agreement or momentary promise. It was a blood covenant even God would not break.

Later, God sent His Son, Jesus Christ, to demonstrate His sacrificial love to all of humanity. The shed blood of Jesus for eternal forgiveness exhibited a Savior who freely loved us from the cross.[3] The scriptures describe the vast reach of this love when it stated that "neither death nor life, neither angels nor demons, neither the present nor the future, nor any powers, neither height nor depth, nor anything else in all creation, will be able to separate us from the love of God that is in Christ Jesus our Lord."[4] His actions were permanent and His purposes selfless as He gave His life freely in covenant love for you and me.

A bride and groom experience the same covenant when they marry. The passing between their family bloodlines demonstrates a covenant has begun. This makes the wedding more than a mere dress up event—it is a lifelong covenant with His blessing.

Even in the sexual intimacy of marriage and then later the birth of covenant children, there is the "passing between" involving a place of blood. This, too, speaks of covenant.

Personally, I believe the covenant and a covenant mindset are what make the difference. Because many do not understand the covenant and its seriousness, homes and relationships simply reflect something of potential value with no long-lasting substance. Loving on purpose, for a purpose, and with purpose is packaged in covenant love. Whether it is from a husband and wife or parents to their children, it is in understanding the covenant walk that makes the difference between noncommitted and forever love.

Covenant eyes are also important, whether you are single or married. Tony and our son, Connor, have made a covenant with their eyes like the passage in the book of Job. Job said, "I made a covenant with my eyes not to look with lust at a young woman," Job 31:1 (NLT). Job's wise and insightful disciplines kept his life and heart focused on good.

The men of our house have a code-word when they are out at a mall or watching a game on television, especially the commercials. Anywhere they may be their accountability to each other is a discipline we ladies of the house admire and appreciate. When the code-word is used, both look away.

Wandering eyes fill the heart with debris, blurring your direction, like the naïve young man in Proverbs chapter seven. A trap was set for him because of his wandering eyes and lack of judgment.

Some women have excused their husbands over the years by saying, "Oh, he has always looked at other women." I have asked them, "How does it make you feel?" They answer me, "I wish he only had eyes for me." Countless women have been forced to compete with pornographic visuals on the computer, magazines and entertainment; consequently, it leaves a woman and a relationship devalued.

A couple committed to work together to protect their marriage sat in the theater watching a movie. As the movie intensified and a compromising scene started to play on the screen, the husband and wife turned to face each other until the questionable scene had passed. Their eyes remained only for one another.

Recently, I was surprised by a young man's confession of something that annoyed him. He had gone to have coffee with his future brother-in-law. While talking together, the potential husband of his sister kept shifting his eyes around, constantly distracted by every woman passing by. Frustrated, the brother asked, "Why do your eyes not meet mine when we talk?" His flippant and defensive answer exposed his heart. "Looking never hurt anyone." His roaming eyes only produced alarm in the brother as he thought about his sister's future. In truth, straying eyes have the potential to hurt many.

Covenant Love

Likewise, many women have also joined the roving eyes club to notice outward appearances and physiques. The outside appearance has never been the gauge for the heart. Outside appearances are temporary and subject to change, but the heart is the core of steadfast love.

In our promiscuous culture, it does not take much to notice the soliciting images of immodesty by just standing in the grocery store lines, not to mention watching television, movies and the internet. The greater discipline is to look away, knowing your heart and eyes belong to another.

Passion is about more than a one-night-stand. Intimacy cannot be forced and authentic love costs something of value. Two hearts given to each other in marriage is more than sexual privilege and pleasure. Protecting your heart as a married person is as essential as protecting your heart as a young single. Since marriage is a covenant, then premarital relationships, or other illicit sex, violates more than one may have considered.

Just like the dating days, some marriages are only honored until one of the partners gets bored or finds another love. Marriage goes beyond a simple contract and is, instead, a lifetime promise under God with witnesses. Our example is the original Covenant Maker who promised never to leave us.[5] His love endures and is steadfast. His eyes are only on His own whom He loves with an everlasting love.[6]

His love, braided with the love of a married couple, offers enduring strength. Truly, "a threefold cord is not easily broken."[7]

Covenant love is devoted and unwavering. It cannot be torn up like an outdated contract nor distracted by other interests. It is eternal love to be esteemed and protected.

A young couple, dedicated to each other and serving the Lord, married one spring. Their devotion to ministry impacted many and their future together was bright as they joined their gifts and talents. In only eight short months their covenant love was tested.

It was during the winter holidays and their house was filled with guests as they spent their first Christmas together. On Christmas Eve they went to bed, lying on their pallets on the floor by the Christmas tree. All the bedrooms were filled with family guests. They did not mind the inconvenience as they purposed to make a memory. They lay under the soft lights of their first Christmas tree while the snow fell quietly outside. Their lives were rich, for the best gift of all was the new love they shared and the expected joy of many holidays yet to come.

That early Christmas morning brought an unexpected package, affecting their lives beyond any surprise. The young wife opened her eyes in the early dawn to discover she could see nothing. In the night her eyes had hemorrhaged without warning.

The young newly-married never mentioned a word to anyone at first because their guests were leaving early to return home from their extended visit. Immediately after the house emptied, the young wife cried out, "I can't see!" Melting in an explosion of tears, she fell into her husband's arms.

Holding her close to his heart, he resolutely said, "We will not retreat."

His words of courage met their new trial with resilient faith and direction toward hope and not fearful defeat.

His declaration, "We will not retreat!" also set the course of the

COVENANT LOVE

young husband's heart. His faithfulness and constant love has never wavered to this day, as he has loved his wife for more than thirty years, in spite of the dark journey and unexpected interruptions.

I know too well the depth of this covenant love. The man who demonstrated such love is my husband, Tony, who has faithfully modeled covenant love throughout the years. Awaking to a blinded bride and resisting the feeling of disappointment, he demonstrated a life-message of one man's selfless, committed love. His love and commitment has aided me in my darkest hour. In the midst of losing my eyesight, vision was birthed. I have seen the evidence of covenant love that has not retreated in the most difficult of times.

Each time my husband offers me his arm, I am his lady of choice and he is my gallant gentleman and life partner. "For better or for worse; for richer or for poorer; in sickness or in health; till death do us part." This is our vow for life.

In spite of all that might come—covenant love never retreats.

Chapter Thirteen
King of Hearts

Cinderella dreams and fantasy love fill you with hope, or perhaps cynicism, depending on whether or not your heart has ever been broken. A little girl imagines her own foot fitting into the glass slipper and marrying her prince charming one day. Another dreams of her knight in shining armor who valiantly swims the mote, scales the wall and slays the dragon to pursue her heart in love.

In contrast, it is said that the way to a man's heart is through his stomach. The stark difference between the romantic and the practical leaves a wide gap.

I wonder if heart issues are considered when matched with childhood fantasies and starlit dreams. Do all love stories end "happily ever after?" If you give your heart to another, will they in return give theirs to you?

In 1981, the royal wedding of lavish dreams played on a stage of nobility with the whole world watching. It is reported that 3,500 guests attended at St. Paul's Cathedral in London, England, to witness the wedding of the century. Nearly 600,000 lined the streets and an estimated 750 million watched by television. Prince Charles of England and Princess Diana of Wales created a majestic wedding ceremony that exceeded all fantasy for the watching audience.

Lady Diana, accompanied by her father, arrived at the Cathedral in a glass carriage. Her ivory taffeta and antique lace gown was

King of Hearts

fitting for a queen. The red-carpeted aisle accentuated the beauty of the Princess's twenty-five-foot-long train. It elegantly flowed behind her during her three-and-a-half-minute walk toward her prince.

Prince Charles, dressed in the formal attire of a naval commander, awaited her at the altar. Even though he muddled his vows and she rearranged his list of given names, the ceremony ended with great pomp and circumstance, resounding for the entire world to hear.

Minutes later, the royal newlyweds embraced on the palace balcony, sharing a kiss. The prince and his lady demonstrated their true love, confirming dreams really do come true. Such a public display of affection by royalty was quite shocking because it never had been seen before.

Sadly, only a few years later, the world was told the royal love story had been dashed by disappointment, depression and tragedy. Two sons were born to the royal couple, but even this joy would satisfy only an agreement for heirs, not proof of devoted love and a happy family.

Shadows of rumors and hints of secret interludes of the prince and his old girlfriend began to appear, much to the dismay of many. In search of companionship and purpose, Lady Diana found new friends and causes to fill her days. Her personable ways and infectious smile won her the title of "Princess of the People." Everyone loved her—except her own prince.

Drastically different is the prophetic love story between an unusual couple of long ago.[1] The man was named Hosea. He was a prophet of God in Northern Israel who was directed of God to marry a woman named Gomer and give her his love. This betrothal of a divine nature, in time, would demonstrate God's message of His

Engaging the Heart

steadfast love and His devoted faithfulness to His people.

Hosea obediently married Gomer, a known prostitute. Amazingly, God gave him a love for this woman of the streets, in spite of her past. They had three children and were instructed to give them specific names. Through the meaning of each child's name, God's message was declared. Gomer soon left her husband to be loved by another man. She returned to her harlot ways, having no regard for her husband's enduring love. Hosea bought her back from the auction-block, redeeming her life with his faithful love.

The marriage of Hosea and Gomer displayed two different hearts. One was of committed love, the other one of straying and unfaithfulness. God's people had turned their back on Him, too. Just like Hosea, God's faithful love to His people has redeemed our lives. Even when we were unlovable and seeking the love of other interests, He loved us unconditionally.[2] He bought back our lives at the auction block of destruction by sending His only Son to die for our sins. Similarly, Jesus Christ demonstrated the Father's love toward us.[3]

To love and be loved has always been the personal choice of mankind. God entrusted us to choose whom we would love.[4] He has chosen, too. However, He has never swerved from his eternal devotion and steadfast love to us. Many have failed to guard their heart, unaware of its value and the issues that will spring up for a lifetime. In living only for the moment, some hearts, tragically, have been given away with no regard of the Savior and of eternity residing in Him.[5] Mistakes from the past leave the heart condemned and calloused to true love. When your heart condemns you, the Savior replies, "I am bigger than all your condemnation."[6] His intentional love far exceeds the past failures of the heart.

Perhaps, as you have read this book, you have revisited wounds and brokenness from your former choices, whether innocent or willful. Jesus still pursues your heart. He is the King of Hearts who loves you, regardless of your history.

Two women of the scriptures were proof of loving beyond their past.

In the course of a simple daily routine, a woman came to a well to draw water. Sitting near the well was a man who spoke to her. He had come from a long journey and was very weary. "Would you give me water to drink?" was his seemingly forward request.[7]

Surprised, but even more puzzled by his question, knowing their cultural differences, she drew water from the well. Diverting from his request, she asked, "Why would you ask me?" Without prejudice and overlooking their differences, the Lord said, "If you only knew the gift of God, then you would ask me for living water. From its wells you would never thirst again."

Tempted by the convenience of never having to come back to the well, she inquired, "What water?" The Lord answered, "Whoever drinks of the water that I shall give him will never thirst. But the water that I shall give him will become in him a fountain of water springing up into everlasting life." She quickly responded, "Give me this water." He then gave the curious directive, "Go get your husband and I will tell you."

"I have no husband," she informed her inquisitor. Jesus responded, affirming what she had said was true. "You have had five husbands and the one you are presently living with is not your own."

Marveling at what He knew, she opened her heart to the One who knew of her past heartache. In spite of her moral failings and broken life, the Lord offered her a cup of new beginnings—His offer of living water from a new eternal spring. Her life message reminds me of Isaiah 12:3, "With joy you will draw from the wells of salvation." Her life was changed and, in telling others, many came to Jesus too.

Do you ever consider the people around you who have shattered dreams and wounded hearts with no hope? Offer them the same cup of living water you have tasted and rejoice together.

Another heartwarming account is of a woman who valued her forgiveness, seeing beyond her tears.[8] Her expression of love to the Savior was beautifully shown by the woman who, in her past, had given her heart and body in prostitution. Her desperate need to do anything in order to be loved and to love had compromised her purity, and the community condemned her actions. However, she now had met her King of Hearts, accepting Him as Lord, and had followed His directive to "sin no more." With a heart of gratitude, she lovingly worshipped, washing her Savior's feet with her tears and wiping them with her hair.

Indignantly, the religious leaders dining with Jesus that day warned, "If only you knew her past." Unmoved by their self-righteousness, a forgiving heart was extended to the woman who worshipped at the feet of her King of Hearts.

Your regrets of yesterday can find solace in the One who cleanses and heals the wounded heart. Jesus publicly proclaimed the heart of His vision and ministry stating, "He has anointed me to preach the gospel to the poor; He has sent me to heal the brokenhearted, to proclaim liberty to the captives and recovery of sight to the blind."[9]

I love His focus for His gospel is good news to all who need forgiveness. His ability heals the broken in heart and liberates the years and memories held captive in your thoughts. Blinded eyes, when opened, see the destiny and plan for His redeeming love. No longer are hearts heavy with grief, but they delight in His heart's desires, experiencing joy and peace. To you who have been disappointed with empty words and fraudulent promises, He is still writing the new chapters of your life. Proverbs encourages us, saying, "Hope deferred makes the heart sick. But when the desire comes, it is like a tree of life."[10] Heartsick pasts are exchanged for promises of new life.

I am captivated by the greatest love story of all—the church being the bride of the Lord.[11] His vows of steadfast love and sacrificial devotion were displayed when He gave Himself willingly on Calvary's cross for His cherished love—you and me. Never did His face turn from pursuing us even when mobs were spitting in His face, plucking out His beard and mocking His motives and name.[12] He remained with covenant eyes as He looked upon us. The book of Hebrews tells us "who for the joy set before Him endured the cross."[13]

Amazingly, we are His eternal joy.

From the beginning of Creation, God demonstrated the cost of enduring love.[14] It was from the side of Adam that Eve was formed from the rib of man, near his heart. Their lives lacked nothing while they lived in a garden of paradise. However, within a short period of time, they broke the heart of their Creator. They had not guarded their hearts; together they disobeyed His instructions. Did they consider the effects on generations yet to come?[15] All mankind now wonders.

While they were left alone with hearts impacted by their choices,

Engaging the Heart

God had already instituted His plan to win them back. Our hearts were lost and without hope, but He exposed His own heart through His Son. He exchanged our brokenness and ruin for wholeness and peace with God, reconciling our hearts to our Creator. Nailed to the cross was our disobedience, exchanged for His obedient life.[16] He exchanged our past for His future, filled with promises to all who would believe. The spotless One offered the final sacrifice for our lives and heart. No greater love has ever been displayed.[17]

Paradise was restored, too, as He offered to us a home with Him. When Jesus went away after His ascension, He proclaimed, like a man of serious courtship, "I go to prepare a place for you."[18]

To the believer, our Bridegroom will return with an explosion of divine romance and valor as He appears on a white stallion[19], swiftly taking His Bride in His arms to take her to His eternal paradise and home. The trumpet will sound and the orchestrated angelic host will sing as the King of the Ages resolutely declares, "You are mine."

Jesus' love was single and focused, yet He knew we would have to choose whom we would love. He opened His heart, taking a risk, freeing us to choose.

To those who have said "Yes" to His love, a wedding feast awaits them. Revelation speaks of the "marriage feast" of the Bride of Christ, His church, and the Lamb, Jesus.[20] In the eternal embrace of committed love, our hearts will be one as we rejoice at the banqueting table.

In your quest for love and a kindred heart, there could be no greater loss than not knowing the Savior. His heart, no matter your past or confusion, yearns for you. His shed blood cleanses the mistakes and renews your joy. [21] He sings over you in the night and pursues you with His forgiving love. [22] His eyes and thoughts are ever on you. His whispers, "You are my love," never end.

My prayer is for you to receive a love of this magnitude by opening your heart to the Lover of your Soul, Jesus Christ. May you, like Gomer, turn from compromised affections and gaze into the eyes of your faithful love and say, "Jesus, I embrace your redeeming love."

He now lovingly extends His life and nail-scarred hands to you, vowing never to leave or forsake you. [23]

Will you receive the King of Hearts?

Will you live every day, engaging your heart with His?

Chapter Fourteen
Is It Too Late?

As you have read this book, *Engaging the Heart*, you may find yourself wondering if it is too late to apply what you have read. It is to you I want to speak.

Perhaps, as you have read the pages, you have felt sadness over never having been challenged to think differently than the culture's way of handling your heart. I remember a young man, nearing his thirties and single, who sat visiting with us in our living room. After talking about heart issues and relationships, he looked at me and said regretfully, "I have never heard of any of this before now. Why didn't anyone tell me?"

Perhaps, you are a parent with grown children, wishing you had known some of these principles while you were raising your family. In fact, you may be tempted to be depressed over lost moments and needless struggles.

I want to comfort you by saying that you walked in the light available to you. And, it is never too late to rebuild your relationship with your children. Phone calls, e-mails and special notes of encouragement can keep doors open as you continue to grow in your relationship.

My dad reminds me that parenting never ends. Your children still have need of your support and encouragement all your life. Your grandchildren need your godly influence and fun memories and

Is It Too Late?

wisdom. It is never too late to capture the hearts of your children. It may, however, take some humility to ask for their forgiveness. Is there a time when you broke their heart or walked away from unresolved conflict? Ask them if you have hurt them unknowingly. Then take the time to listen and reaffirm your love to them. Pray together, if possible. Embrace them as you validate your love.

Be motivated by the success you are hoping for the next generation as you resolve conflict and work toward righteous conclusions. Too much is at stake to do otherwise.

Often we are told, "I wish you were my parents." I thank them for the compliment and then laugh as I say they might want to check with our children. We, too, are just normal parents. Our vision is to gain our children's hearts. We are passionate about their success and believe God is the One who will fulfill their purpose in their generation.

Maybe your parents are reluctant to actively involve themselves in the heart issues of your life. Possibly, their hesitation is because they don't know what to do. If you have shared with them and they are unable or unwilling to involve themselves in issues of the heart, then find mentors and Christian leaders who *are* willing. Don't bear a grudge toward your parents for not walking in light they have never seen. Perhaps the truth and the principles you now embrace were never cultivated or modeled to them. Honor them just the same. They gave you life. You can now maximize your life with God's power and love.

A college age girl stood before me weeping over her relationship with her father. I began to hug her as she soaked my shoulder with her tears as she said, "God has begun to heal my relationship with my dad, but he can never be what I need for this season in my life." The past years of abuse and broken trust by the father she had longed for and needed had created a gulf not easily bridged. Though she had forgiven him and was making attempts to rebuild the relationship, the tears of disappointment were intertwined with regret *and* determination.

Lifting her head with resolve, she said, "I will be a generation breaker." Though the term was unfamiliar to me, I clearly understood her heart. She was announcing that her tomorrows *must* be different from what she had experienced as a child. Her vision and faith were now set on working to make things different for her husband and children yet to come. I stood grieved by the needless heartache a daughter should have with a father. Calling her by name, I said, "Then one of the most essential questions that must be asked of your suitors is, 'Do you have the courage it takes to be a generation breaker with me and build a safe home for our future family?'"

Vision for tomorrow will help heal the oversights of yesterday.

To those who have lost their virginity, whether willingly or it was stolen, I remind you that He is the Great Redeemer. He alone can redeem innocence. His forgiveness is as far as the east is from the west. He is faithful and just to forgive. And his blood washes you white as snow. His work at Calvary is your hope and triumph. His beginnings are new.

The caterpillar reminds us that His changes are complete. "Old things have passed away…all things have become new."[1] Ask Him to make you new. The cocoon is open as you take flight into a new pure journey where His ways delight you and His paths are filled with new life.

Is It Too Late?

Any regrets? Jesus said, "Now is the day of salvation." Rejoice in what you know today and ask Him to restore your yesterday. Remain teachable as you reach for more of Him. Commit to teach the next generation from your developing life-message.

To the most puzzled of all—the parents who taught their children well and yet their children chose to take a difficult path—quit condemning yourself. Love is about free choices. Your greatest challenge for this moment is to demonstrate His grace and love as you pray, believing. Truly care for the safety of your child's life and corresponding consequences. But don't be consumed in how it may look to others. You have not failed. Release yourself to walk in a level of love you have never known. Position yourself on the porch like the father of the prodigal son. The father of that stirring story watched in hope for his son to return. God does the same with us.

Innocence, purity and virtue can be restored by the Savior. Ask Him.

Hope and vision can be birthed as you open your mind to walk in His principles and not in the way of our culture. There is a more excellent way.

When your heart condemns you, God is greater than your heart. Can you trust the Savior to take your shattered pieces and make you whole again? When the Lord heals it is without scars. Ask Him. He knows all things.

Don't continue looking in the rear view mirror of your life with past regrets and longing. Allow the Lord to use your life-message to help others who cannot see His forgiving grace.

Possibly, the most damaging conditions of all are past heart failures. If your life has been scarred by broken relationships, learn and change. "God is working in you, giving you the desire and the power to do what pleases Him" (Philippians 2:13, NLT). Don't let disappointments from the past blind you from the hope available today.

Don't mistake the dark places as abandonment. Psalm 91 reminds us we dwell under His shadow.[2] God has never left you alone. Your past wounds may be inflamed because of accusations, insults and rejection. The Savior, too, was rejected by all men and mocked by those who misunderstood. He will comfort you as He alone can work all things for good.

If you have been the one who has wounded others by your words and actions, humble yourself as you earnestly ask for their forgiveness and His. Choose to walk a higher road, placing your anger and expectations under His lordship.

Treasuring your heart and the hearts of others is a noble choice. The Lord Himself will meet you at every turn in the road. Just ask.

Do you feel like you are alone and you are the only one with a vision for your children? Are you a single parent concerned you cannot prepare your child adequately? May I encourage you about a young man in the scriptures who influenced many, in spite of his young age? He, too, only had a mother and grandmother who trained him, yet his life produced greatness as the apostle Paul took the young Timothy under his wing.[3] God can work in the middle of less than perfect situations. The Lord will bring the support you need.

To those who walk alone in their marriage, with no evidence of intimacy or shared vision with their spouse, I say to you to let hope live again as you determine never to give up. God can breathe on the dry bones of your marriage and cause life to come again.

Is It Too Late?

God promised to be a father to the orphans.[4] His heart is to place the isolated in a family. He said He would be the husband to the widow.[5] His wisdom is offered liberally and He is your protection. Romans states, "If God be for you, who can be against you?"[6] He is near to all who call upon Him—simply call.[7]

What would keep your heart from engaging with His in this moment? Pray with me...

Dear Jesus, I surrender my heart to you. Thank you that you are the Redeemer and Restorer of my life.

I desire authentic love. Show me how to love. Grace me with courage to keep my heart with all diligence. Let the issues flowing from my life-message influence others in my generation to live for You.

Release me to walk in the destiny You desire for my life and to fulfill all Your purposes.

I readily give You my heart—trusting. Please forgive me for all my sins. I confess Jesus as my Lord and believe God has raised Him from the dead. I choose You, Jesus Christ.

Thank you, Lord, for freeing my heart from condemnation. Renew it once again to remain open and alive in you. May I have courage as I walk in Your wisdom.

I engage my heart in Yours.

Access the Free Bonus Chapter On-Line!

To access Gail's bonus chapter to *Engaging the Heart* go to
www.BonusChapter.com

End Notes

All scriptures are from the New King James Version except where noted.

Engaging the Heart

Preface From the Stroller

Introduction Game of Hearts

Chapter 1 Who Has Your Heart?

[1] Proverbs 22:15 *"Foolishness is bound up in the heart of a child; the rod of correction will drive it far from him."*

[2] See You at the Top; Author, Zig Ziglar; ©1975, 1977, 2000; Publisher, Pelican Publishing Company.

[3] Normal is Just a Setting on Your Dryer; *Author, Patsy Clairmont; ©1999; Publisher, Tyndale House Publishers.*

Chapter 2 Cup of Purity

[1] Mrs. Rosey-Posey and the Chocolate Cherry Treat; *author; Robin Jones Gunn, ©1991; Illustrator, Bill Duca, ChariotVictor Publishing. This book has since been republished under Mrs. Rosey Posey and the Fine China Plate; ©2008; Publisher, ZonderKids*

[2] Psalm 16:5 *"O LORD, You are the portion of my inheritance and my cup; You maintain my lot."*

[3] Proverbs 23:7 *"For as he thinks in his heart, so is he."*

[4] Psalm 24:4-5 *"He who has clean hands and a pure heart, who has not lifted up his soul to an idol, nor sworn deceitfully. ⁵ He shall receive blessing from the LORD, and righteousness from the God of his salvation."*

End Notes

Chapter 3   The Blessing

[1] The Father's Blessing; *Author/Teacher, William T. Ligon, Sr.; www. TheFathersBlessing.com.*

[2] Matthew 19:13 *"Then little children were brought to Him that He might put His hands on them and pray, but the deciples rebuked them."*

Chapter 4   Sleeping Beauty

[1] Ecclesiastes 4:12 *"Though one may be overpowered by another, two can withstand him. And a threefold cord is not quickly broken."*

Chapter 5   Secret Garden

[1] Song of Solomon 4:12-16 *"A garden enclosed is my sister, my spouse, A spring shut up, A fountain sealed.* [13] *Your plants are an orchard of pomegranates with pleasant fruits, fragrant henna with spikenard,* [14] *spikenard and saffron, calamus and cinnamon, with all trees of frankincense, myrrh and aloes, with all the chief spices—* [15] *a fountain of gardens, a well of living waters, and streams from Lebanon. The Shulamite* [16] *Awake, O north wind, and come, O south! Blow upon my garden, that its spices may flow out. Let my beloved come to his garden and eat its pleasant fruits."*

Chapter 6   The Impostor

[1] Hebrews 13:5 *"Let your conduct be without covetousness; be content with such things as you have. For He Himself has said, 'I will never leave you nor forsake you.'"*

[2] 2 Timothy 3:13 *"But evil men and impostors will grow worse and worse, deceiving and being deceived."*

Chapter 7 No Secrets—No Lies

[1] **John 14:6** *"Jesus said to him, "I am the way, the truth, and the life. No one comes to the Father except through Me."*

[2] **2 Corinthians 6:14** *"Do not be unequally yoked together with unbelievers. For what fellowship has righteousness with lawlessness? And what communion has light with darkness?"*

Chapter 8 Crowded Altar

[1] **Hebrews 11:25** *"choosing rather to suffer affliction with the people of God than to enjoy the passing pleasures of sin,"*

[2] **Psalm 103:12** *"As far as the east is from the west, so far has He removed our transgressions from us."*

[3] **I John 1:9** *"If we confess our sins, He is faithful and just to forgive us our sins and to cleanse us from all unrighteousness."*

[4] **Proverbs 4:18** *"But the path of the just is like the shining sun, that shines ever brighter unto the perfect day."*

[5] **Romans 8:39** *"nor height nor depth, nor any other created thing, shall be able to separate us from the love of God which is in Christ Jesus our Lord."*

[6] **I John 1:9** *"If we confess our sins, He is faithful and just to forgive us our sins and to cleanse us from all unrighteousness."*

[7] **Romans 10:9** *"that if you confess with your mouth the Lord Jesus and believe in your heart that God has raised Him from the dead, you will be saved."*

[8] **Hebrews 13:5** *"Let your conduct be without covetousness; be content with

End Notes

such things as you have. For He Himself has said, 'I will never leave you nor forsake you.'"

⁹ Psalms 91:1, 2 *"He who dwells in the secret place of the Most High shall abide under the shadow of the Almighty. ²I will say of the LORD, 'He is my refuge and my fortress; My God, in Him I will trust.'"*

Chapter 9   Heart Strings

¹ Proverbs 13:20 *"He who walks with wise men will be wise, but the companion of fools will be destroyed."*.

² Proverbs 17:17 *"A friend loves at all times, and a brother is born for adversity."*

³ Guard Your Heart; Words and Music, Jon Mohr; Composed, 1989; Publisher, EMI Christian Music Publishing.

⁴ John 14:14 *"If you ask anything in My name, I will do it."*

Chapter 10   The Exchange

¹ Genesis 29:14-30 *"And Laban said to him, "Surely you are my bone and my flesh." And he stayed with him for a month. ¹⁵ Then Laban said to Jacob, "Because you are my relative, should you therefore serve me for nothing? Tell me, what should your wages be?" ¹⁶ Now Laban had two daughters: the name of the elder was Leah, and the name of the younger was Rachel. ¹⁷ Leah's eyes were delicate, but Rachel was beautiful of form and appearance. ¹⁸ Now Jacob loved Rachel; so he said, "I will serve you seven years for Rachel your younger daughter." ¹⁹ And Laban said, "It is better that I give her to you than that I should give her to another man. Stay with me." ²⁰ So Jacob served seven years for Rachel, and they seemed only a few days to him because of the love he had for her. ²¹ Then Jacob said to Laban, "Give me my wife, for my days are fulfilled, that I may go in to her." ²² And Laban gathered together all the men of the place and made a feast. ²³ Now it came to pass in the evening, that he took*

Engaging the Heart

Leah his daughter and brought her to Jacob; and he went in to her. ²⁴ And Laban gave his maid Zilpah to his daughter Leah as a maid. ²⁵ So it came to pass in the morning, that behold, it was Leah. And he said to Laban, "What is this you have done to me? Was it not for Rachel that I served you? Why then have you deceived me?" ²⁶ And Laban said, "It must not be done so in our country, to give the younger before the firstborn. ²⁷ Fulfill her week, and we will give you this one also for the service which you will serve with me still another seven years." ²⁸ Then Jacob did so and fulfilled her week. So he gave him his daughter Rachel as wife also. ²⁹ And Laban gave his maid Bilhah to his daughter Rachel as a maid. ³⁰ Then Jacob also went in to Rachel, and he also loved Rachel more than Leah. And he served with Laban still another seven years.

² I Like You; *Author, Sandol Stoddard, ©1993 Renewed; Illustrator, Jacqueline Chwarst; ©1993 Renewed; Publisher, Houghton Mifflin Company.*

Chapter 11 The Kiss

¹ Proverbs 6:27 *"Can a man take fire to his bosom, and his clothes not be burned?"*

² Numbers 6:24-26 *"The LORD bless you and keep you; 25 the LORD make His face shine upon you, and be gracious to you; 26 the LORD lift up His countenance upon you, and give you peace."*

³ Romans 8:28 *"And we know that all things work together for good to those who love God, to those who are the called according to His purpose."*

⁴ Deuteronomy 32:30 *"How could one chase a thousand, and two put ten thousand to flight, unless their Rock had sold them, and the LORD had surrendered them?"*

⁵ Psalm 20:4 *"May He grant you according to your heart's desire, and fulfill all your purpose."*

End Notes

Chapter 12   Covenant Love

[1] Scarred; *Author/Speaker, Dave Roever, ©1995; Publisher, Roever Communications; www.DaveRoever.org*

[2] Genesis 15:1-21 *After these things the word of the LORD came to Abram in a vision, saying, "Do not be afraid, Abram. I am your shield, your exceedingly great reward."* [2] *But Abram said, "Lord GOD, what will You give me, seeing I go childless, and the heir of my house is Eliezer of Damascus?"* [3] *Then Abram said, "Look, You have given me no offspring; indeed one born in my house is my heir!"* [4] *And behold, the word of the LORD came to him, saying, "This one shall not be your heir, but one who will come from your own body shall be your heir."* [5] *Then He brought him outside and said, "Look now toward heaven, and count the stars if you are able to number them." And He said to him, "So shall your descendants be."* [6] *And he believed in the LORD, and He accounted it to him for righteousness.* [7] *Then He said to him, "I am the LORD, who brought you out of Ur of the Chaldeans, to give you this land to inherit it."* [8] *And he said, "Lord GOD, how shall I know that I will inherit it?"* [9] *So He said to him, "Bring Me a three-year-old heifer, a three-year-old female goat, a three-year-old ram, a turtledove, and a young pigeon."* [10] *Then he brought all these to Him and cut them in two, down the middle, and placed each piece opposite the other; but he did not cut the birds in two.* [11] *And when the vultures came down on the carcasses, Abram drove them away.* [12] *Now when the sun was going down, a deep sleep fell upon Abram; and behold, horror and great darkness fell upon him.* [13] *Then He said to Abram: "Know certainly that your descendants will be strangers in a land that is not theirs, and will serve them, and they will afflict them four hundred years.* [14] *And also the nation whom they serve I will judge; afterward they shall come out with great possessions.* [15] *Now as for you, you shall go to your fathers in peace; you shall be buried at a good old age.* [16] *But in the fourth generation they shall return here, for the iniquity of the Amorites is not yet complete."* [17] *And it came to pass, when the sun went down and it was dark, that behold, there appeared a smoking oven and a burning torch that passed between those pieces.* [18] *On the same day the LORD made a covenant with Abram, saying: "To your descendants I have given this land, from the river of Egypt to the great river, the River Euphrates—* [19]

the Kenites, the Kenezzites, the Kadmonites, [20] the Hittites, the Perizzites, the Rephaim, 21 the Amorites, the Canaanites, the Girgashites, and the Jebusites.".

[3] **Hebrews 9:11-14** *But Christ came as High Priest of the good things to come, with the greater and more perfect tabernacle not made with hands, that is, not of this creation.* [12] *Not with the blood of goats and calves, but with His own blood He entered the Most Holy Place once for all, having obtained eternal redemption.* [13] *For if the blood of bulls and goats and the ashes of a heifer, sprinkling the unclean, sanctifies for the purifying of the flesh,* [14] *how much more shall the blood of Christ, who through the eternal Spirit offered Himself without spot to God, cleanse your conscience from dead works to serve the living God?*
Luke 23:33 *And when they had come to the place called Calvary, there they crucified Him, and the criminals, one on the right hand and the other on the left.*
John 15:13 *Greater love has no one than this, than to lay down one's life for his friends.*

[4] **Romans 8:39** *"nor height nor depth, nor any other created thing, shall be able to separate us from the love of God which is in Christ Jesus our Lord."*

[5] **Hebrews 13:5** *Let your conduct be without covetousness; be content with such things as you have. For He Himself has said, "I will never leave you nor forsake you."*

[6] **Jeremiah 31:3** *"The LORD has appeared of old to me, saying: 'Yes, I have loved you with an everlasting love; therefore with loving kindness I have drawn you'"*

[7] **Ecclesiastes 4:12** *"Though one may be overpowered by another, two can withstand him. And a threefold cord is not quickly broken."*

Chapter 13   King of Hearts

[1] **Hosea Chapter 1** *"The word of the LORD that came to Hosea the son of*

End Notes

Beeri, in the days of Uzziah, Jotham, Ahaz, and Hezekiah, kings of Judah, and in the days of Jeroboam the son of Joash, king of Israel. [2] When the LORD began to speak by Hosea, the LORD said to Hosea: 'Go, take yourself a wife of harlotry and children of harlotry, for the land has committed great harlotry by departing from the LORD.' [3] So he went and took Gomer the daughter of Diblaim, and she conceived and bore him a son. [4] Then the LORD said to him: 'Call his name Jezreel', for in a little while I will avenge the bloodshed of Jezreel on the house of Jehu, and bring an end to the kingdom of the house of Israel. [5] It shall come to pass in that day that I will break the bow of Israel in the Valley of Jezreel.' [6] And she conceived again and bore a daughter. Then God said to him: 'Call her name Lo-Ruhamah, for I will no longer have mercy on the house of Israel, but I will utterly take them away. [7] Yet I will have mercy on the house of Judah, will save them by the LORD their God, and will not save them by bow, nor by sword or battle, by horses or horsemen.' [8] Now when she had weaned Lo-Ruhamah, she conceived and bore a son. [9] Then God said: 'Call his name Lo-Ammi', for you are not My people, and I will not be your God.[10] "Yet the number of the children of Israel shall be as the sand of the sea, which cannot be measured or numbered. And it shall come to pass in the place where it was said to them, 'You are not My people,' there it shall be said to them, 'You are sons of the living God.' [11] Then the children of Judah and the children of Israel shall be gathered together, and appoint for themselves one head; and they shall come up out of the land, for great will be the day of Jezreel!";

Hosea Chapter 3 *"Then the LORD said to me, 'Go again, love a woman who is loved by a lover and is committing adultery, just like the love of the LORD for the children of Israel, who look to others gods and love the raisin cakes of the pagans.' [2] So I bought her for myself for fifteen shekels of silver, and one and one-half homers of barley.[3] And I said to her, 'You shall stay with me many days; you shall not play the harlot, nor shall you have a man—so, too, will I be toward you.' [4] For the children of Israel shall abide many days without king or prince, without sacrifice or sacred pillar, without ephod or teraphim. [5] Afterward the children of Israel shall return and seek the LORD their God and David their king. They shall fear the LORD and His goodness in the latter days."*

Engaging the Heart

[2] **Romans 5:8** *"But God demonstrates His own love toward us, in that while we were still sinners, Christ died for us."*

[3] **Revelation 5:9** *"And they sang a new song, saying: ' You are worthy to take the scroll, and to open its seals; for You were slain, and have redeemed us to God by Your blood out of every tribe and tongue and people and nation,";*
I John 4:9,10 *"In this the love of God was manifested toward us, that God has sent His only begotten Son into the world, that we might live through Him.* [10] *In this is love, not that we loved God, but that He loved us and sent His Son to be the propitiation for our sins."*

[4] **Joshua 24:15** *"And if it seems evil to you to serve the LORD, choose for yourselves this day whom you will serve, whether the gods which your fathers served that were on the other side of the River, or the gods of the Amorites, in whose land you dwell. But as for me and my house, we will serve the LORD."*

[5] **Ecclesiastes 3:11** *"He has made everything beautiful in its time. Also He has put eternity in their hearts, except that no one can find out the work that God does from beginning to end."*

[6] **1 John 3:20** *"For if our heart condemns us, God is greater than our heart, and knows all things."*

[7] **John 4:4-42** *"But He needed to go through Samaria.*[5] *So He came to a city of Samaria which is called Sychar, near the plot of ground that Jacob gave to his son Joseph.* [6] *Now Jacob's well was there. Jesus therefore, being wearied from His journey, sat thus by the well. It was about the sixth hour.* [7] *A woman of Samaria came to draw water. Jesus said to her, "Give Me a drink."* [8] *For His disciples had gone away into the city to buy food.* [9] *Then the woman of Samaria said to Him, "How is it that You, being a Jew, ask a drink from me, a Samaritan woman?" For Jews have no dealings with Samaritans.* [10] *Jesus answered and said to her, "If you knew the gift of God, and who it is who says to you, 'Give Me a drink,' you would have asked Him, and He would have given you living water."* [11] *The woman said*

End Notes

to Him, "Sir, You have nothing to draw with, and the well is deep. Where then do You get that living water? [12] Are You greater than our father Jacob, who gave us the well, and drank from it himself, as well as his sons and his livestock?" [13] Jesus answered and said to her, "Whoever drinks of this water will thirst again, [14] but whoever drinks of the water that I shall give him will never thirst. But the water that I shall give him will become in him a fountain of water springing up into everlasting life." [15] The woman said to Him, "Sir, give me this water, that I may not thirst, nor come here to draw." [16] Jesus said to her, "Go, call your husband, and come here." [17] The woman answered and said, "I have no husband." Jesus said to her, "You have well said, 'I have no husband,' [18] for you have had five husbands, and the one whom you now have is not your husband; in that you spoke truly." [19] The woman said to Him, "Sir, I perceive that You are a prophet. [20] Our fathers worshiped on this mountain, and you Jews say that in Jerusalem is the place where one ought to worship." [21] Jesus said to her, "Woman, believe Me, the hour is coming when you will neither on this mountain, nor in Jerusalem, worship the Father. [22] You worship what you do not know; we know what we worship, for salvation is of the Jews. [23] But the hour is coming, and now is, when the true worshipers will worship the Father in spirit and truth; for the Father is seeking such to worship Him. [24] God is Spirit, and those who worship Him must worship in spirit and truth." [25] The woman said to Him, "I know that Messiah is coming" (who is called Christ). "When He comes, He will tell us all things." [26] Jesus said to her, "I who speak to you am He." [27] And at this point His disciples came, and they marveled that He talked with a woman; yet no one said, "What do You seek?" or, "Why are You talking with her?" [28] The woman then left her water pot, went her way into the city, and said to the men, [29] "Come, see a Man who told me all things that I ever did. Could this be the Christ?" [30] Then they went out of the city and came to Him. [31] In the meantime His disciples urged Him, saying, "Rabbi, eat." [32] But He said to them, "I have food to eat of which you do not know." [33] Therefore the disciples said to one another, "Has anyone brought Him anything to eat?" [34] Jesus said to them, "My food is to do the will of Him who sent Me, and to finish His work. [35] Do you not say, 'There are still four months and then comes the harvest'? Behold, I say to you, lift up your eyes and look at the fields, for they are already white for harvest! [36] And he who reaps receives wages, and gathers fruit

Engaging the Heart

for eternal life, that both he who sows and he who reaps may rejoice together. [37] For in this the saying is true: 'One sows and another reaps.' [38] I sent you to reap that for which you have not labored; others have labored, and you have entered into their labors." [39] And many of the Samaritans of that city believed in Him because of the word of the woman who testified, "He told me all that I ever did." [40] So when the Samaritans had come to Him, they urged Him to stay with them; and He stayed there two days. [41] And many more believed because of His own word. [42] Then they said to the woman, "Now we believe, not because of what you said, for we ourselves have heard Him and we know that this is indeed the Christ, the Savior of the world."

[8] **Luke 7:36-50** *"Then one of the Pharisees asked Him to eat with him. And He went to the Pharisee's house, and sat down to eat. [37] And behold, a woman in the city who was a sinner, when she knew that Jesus sat at the table in the Pharisee's house, brought an alabaster flask of fragrant oil, [38] and stood at His feet behind Him weeping; and she began to wash His feet with her tears, and wiped them with the hair of her head; and she kissed His feet and anointed them with the fragrant oil. [39] Now when the Pharisee who had invited Him saw this, he spoke to himself, saying, "This Man, if He were a prophet, would know who and what manner of woman this is who is touching Him, for she is a sinner." [40] And Jesus answered and said to him, "Simon, I have something to say to you." So he said, "Teacher, say it." [41] "There was a certain creditor who had two debtors. One owed five hundred denarii, and the other fifty. [42] And when they had nothing with which to repay, he freely forgave them both. Tell Me, therefore, which of them will love him more?" [43] Simon answered and said, "I suppose the one whom he forgave more." And He said to him, "You have rightly judged." [44] Then He turned to the woman and said to Simon, "Do you see this woman? I entered your house; you gave Me no water for My feet, but she has washed My feet with her tears and wiped them with the hair of her head. [45] You gave Me no kiss, but this woman has not ceased to kiss My feet since the time I came in. [46] You did not anoint My head with oil, but this woman has anointed My feet with fragrant oil. [47] Therefore I say to you, her sins, which are many, are forgiven, for she loved much. But to whom little is forgiven, the same loves little." [48] Then He said to her, "Your sins are forgiven."*

End Notes

[49] *And those who sat at the table with Him began to say to themselves, "Who is this who even forgives sins?"* [50] *Then He said to the woman, "Your faith has saved you. Go in peace."*

[9] Luke 4:18 *"The Spirit of the LORD is upon Me, because He has anointed Me to preach the gospel to the poor; He has sent Me to heal the brokenhearted, to proclaim liberty to the captives and recovery of sight to the blind, to set at liberty those who are oppressed;"*

[10] Proverbs 13:12 *"Hope deferred makes the heart sick, but when the desire comes, it is a tree of life."*

[11] Ephesians 5:23-25 *"For the husband is head of the wife, as also Christ is head of the church; and He is the Savior of the body.* [24] *Therefore, just as the church is subject to Christ, so let the wives be to their own husbands in everything.* [25] *Husbands, love your wives, just as Christ also loved the church and gave Himself for her,"*

[12] Isaiah 50:6 *"I gave My back to those who struck Me, and My cheeks to those who plucked out the beard; I did not hide My face from shame and spitting."*

[13] Hebrews 12:2 *"looking unto Jesus, the author and finisher of our faith, who for the joy that was set before Him endured the cross, despising the shame, and has sat down at the right hand of the throne of God."*

[14] Genesis 2:21-3:24 *"And the LORD God caused a deep sleep to fall on Adam, and he slept; and He took one of his ribs, and closed up the flesh in its place.* [22] *Then the rib which the LORD God had taken from man He made into a woman, and He brought her to the man.* [23] *And Adam said: 'This is now bone of my bones and flesh of my flesh; She shall be called woman, because she was taken out of Man.'* [24] *Therefore a man shall leave his father and mother and be joined to his wife, and they shall become one flesh.* [25] *And they were both naked, the man and his wife, and were not ashamed. 3:* [1] *Now the serpent was more cunning*

Engaging the Heart

than any beast of the field which the LORD God had made. And he said to the woman, Has God indeed said, 'You shall not eat of every tree of the garden'? [2] And the woman said to the serpent, 'We may eat the fruit of the trees of the garden; [3] but of the fruit of the tree which is in the midst of the garden, God has said, 'You shall not eat it, nor shall you touch it, lest you die.'" [4] Then the serpent said to the woman, 'You will not surely die. [5] For God knows that in the day you eat of it your eyes will be opened, and you will be like God, knowing good and evil." [6] So when the woman saw that the tree was good for food, that it was pleasant to the eyes, and a tree desirable to make one wise, she took of its fruit and ate. She also gave to her husband with her, and he ate. [7] Then the eyes of both of them were opened, and they knew that they were naked; and they sewed fig leaves together and made themselves coverings. [8] And they heard the sound of the LORD God walking in the garden in the cool of the day, and Adam and his wife hid themselves from the presence of the LORD God among the trees of the garden. [9] Then the LORD God called to Adam and said to him, 'Where are you?' [10] So he said, "I heard Your voice in the garden, and I was afraid because I was naked; and I hid myself." [11] And He said, "Who told you that you were naked? Have you eaten from the tree of which I commanded you that you should not eat?" [12] Then the man said, "The woman whom You gave to be with me, she gave me of the tree, and I ate." [13] And the LORD God said to the woman, "What is this you have done?" The woman said, "The serpent deceived me, and I ate." [14] So the LORD God said to the serpent: " Because you have done this, You are cursed more than all cattle, And more than every beast of the field; On your belly you shall go, And you shall eat dust All the days of your life. [15] And I will put enmity between you and the woman, and between your seed and her Seed; He shall bruise your head, and you shall bruise His heel." [16] To the woman He said: "I will greatly multiply your sorrow and your conception; In pain you shall bring forth children; Your desire shall be for your husband, And he shall rule over you." [17] Then to Adam He said, "Because you have heeded the voice of your wife, and have eaten from the tree of which I commanded you, saying, 'You shall not eat of it': "Cursed is the ground for your sake; In toil you shall eat of it all the days of your life.[18] Both thorns and thistles it shall bring forth for you, and you shall eat the herb of the field. [19] In the sweat of your face you shall eat

End Notes

bread till you return to the ground, for out of it you were taken; for dust you are, and to dust you shall return." [20] And Adam called his wife's name Eve, because she was the mother of all living. [21] Also for Adam and his wife the LORD God made tunics of skin, and clothed them. [22] Then the LORD God said, "Behold, the man has become like one of Us, to know good and evil. And now, lest he put out his hand and take also of the tree of life, and eat, and live forever" — [23] therefore the LORD God sent him out of the garden of Eden to till the ground from which he was taken. [24] So He drove out the man; and He placed cherubim at the east of the garden of Eden, and a flaming sword which turned every way, to guard the way to the tree of life."

[15] **Romans 5:12** *"Therefore, just as through one man sin entered the world, and death through sin, and thus death spread to all men, because all sinned."*

[16] **Colossians 2:13-15** *"And you, being dead in your trespasses and the uncircumcision of your flesh, He has made alive together with Him, having forgiven you all trespasses, [14] having wiped out the handwriting of requirements that was against us, which was contrary to us. And He has taken it out of the way, having nailed it to the cross. [15] Having disarmed principalities and powers, He made a public spectacle of them, triumphing over them in it."*

[17] **John 15:13** *"Greater love has no one than this, than to lay down one's life for his friends."*

[18] **John 14:1-4** *"Let not your heart be troubled; you believe in God, believe also in Me. [2] In My Father's house are many mansions; if it were not so, I would have told you. I go to prepare a place for you. [3] And if I go and prepare a place for you, I will come again and receive you to Myself; that where I am, there you may be also. [4] And where I go you know, and the way you know."*

[19] **Revelation 19:11** *"Now I saw heaven opened, and behold, a white horse. And He who sat on him was called Faithful and True, and in righteousness He judges and makes war."*

Engaging the Heart

[20] **Revelation 19:7-9** *"Let us be glad and rejoice and give Him glory, for the marriage of the Lamb has come, and His wife has made herself ready."* [8] *And to her it was granted to be arrayed in fine linen, clean and bright, for the fine linen is the righteous acts of the saints. Then he said to me, "Write: 'Blessed are those who are called to the marriage supper of the Lamb!'" And he said to me, "These are the true sayings of God."*

[21] **John 15:11** *"These things I have spoken to you, that My joy may remain in you, and that your joy may be full."*
1 Peter 1:8 *"whom having not seen you love. Though now you do not see Him, yet believing, you rejoice with joy inexpressible and full of glory,*

[22] **Zephaniah 3:17"** *The LORD your God in your midst, the Mighty One, will save; He will rejoice over you with gladness, He will quiet you with His love, He will rejoice over you with singing."*

[23] **Hebrews 13:5** *"Let your conduct be without covetousness; be content with such things as you have. For He Himself has said, "I will never leave you nor forsake you."*

Chapter 14   Is It Too Late?

[1] **2 Corinthians 5:17** *"Therefore, if anyone is in Christ, he is a new creation; old things have passed away; behold, all things have become new.*

[2] **Psalm 91:1** *"He who dwells in the secret place of the Most High, shall abide under the shadow of the Almighty."*

[3] **2 Timothy 1:5** *"when I call to remembrance the genuine faith that is in you, which dwelt first in your grandmother Lois and your mother Eunice, and I am persuaded is in you also."*

[4] **John 14:18** *"I will not leave you orphans; I will come to you."*

End Notes

[5] Isaiah 54:4-5 *" Do not fear, for you will not be ashamed; neither be disgraced, for you will not be put to shame; for you will forget the shame of your youth, and will not remember the reproach of your widowhood anymore. [5] For your Maker is your husband, The LORD of hosts is His name; and your redeemer is the Holy One of Israel; He is called the God of the whole earth."*

[6] Romans 8:31 *"What then shall we say to these things If God is for us, who can be against us?"*

[7] Psalm 145:18 *"The LORD is near to all who call upon Him, to all who call upon Him in truth."*

About The Author

Gail McWilliams has an instinctive ability to capture and lift the spirits of people, empowering them for a renewed reach toward dreams and purpose they once thought impossible. She has a vivacious personality, effervescent humor and an uncanny capacity to deliver her life-message. No wonder Gail is met with such broad and energetic approval across the nation as she delivers penetrating inspiration, motivating audiences to ascend new summits.

Her love is people and her passion is leaders. Gail's versatility generates invitations from a wide variety of organizations where she effectively customizes her life-message to benefit any audience, leaving them inspired and motivated. She couples courage with a joyful determination to seize every day for good and blaze a triumphant trail for others to follow. She has extensive experience in public speaking, television and radio, as a recording artist and life-coach, and is a compelling author.

Her first book, *Seeing Beyond: Choosing to Look Past the Horizon*, with foreword by Zig Ziglar, captured the attention of people worldwide, leaving them wanting more.

She is a wife, mother, and grandmother and resides in Texas.

Contact the Author

Gail McWilliams can be contacted for bookings at
www.GailMcWilliams.com

Access the Free Bonus Chapter On-Line!

To access Gail's bonus chapter to *Engaging the Heart* go to
www.BonusChapter.com

Seeing Beyond
Choosing to Look Past the Horizon
By Gail McWilliams

Order this book and related products at
www.GailMcWilliams.com